Blockchain Consensus For Grid Defense

By
Gissah

CHAPTER **TITLE** **PAGE NO.**

TABLE OF CONTENTS

CHAPTER 1

INTRODUCTION

1.1. Introduction

Nowadays, society has been characterised by a growing dependency on digital systems, which, while offering unprecedented efficiencies, simultaneously introduce complex vulnerabilities, particularly in critical infrastructure like power grids. The thesis directly addresses this dichotomy by proposing a novel solution rooted in blockchain technology. While blockchain is often associated with cryptocurrencies, its core attributes decentralization, immutability, and tamper-proof data management extend far beyond finance, offering a robust paradigm for enhancing cybersecurity. This research posits that by leveraging a blockchain-based framework, it is possible to safeguard the integrity and resilience of power grid information, specifically against the insidious threat of fifty one percent cyber-attacks. Despite these challenges, there is potential for Blockchain to be complemented by other emerging technologies to address its vulnerabilities [1]. This introduction will not merely delve into the general concepts of blockchain but will specifically frame its relevance within the context of securing vital energy infrastructures from sophisticated digital threats, laying the groundwork for a detailed exploration of the proposed framework.

1.2. Blockchain Technology

Stuart Haber and W. Scott Stornetta first introduced the idea of securing a blockchain in 1991. In 2008, someone or a group using the name "Satoshi Nakamoto" changed everything by introducing blockchain technology with Bitcoin, which was the very first cryptocurrency. Nakamoto's innovation involved using cryptographic hashing to ensure that once a record is stored in the blockchain, it is immutable meaning that no one can alter or remove it without the consensus of the entire network. Fig.1.1 illustrates the structure of a blockchain, showing how each block is connected.

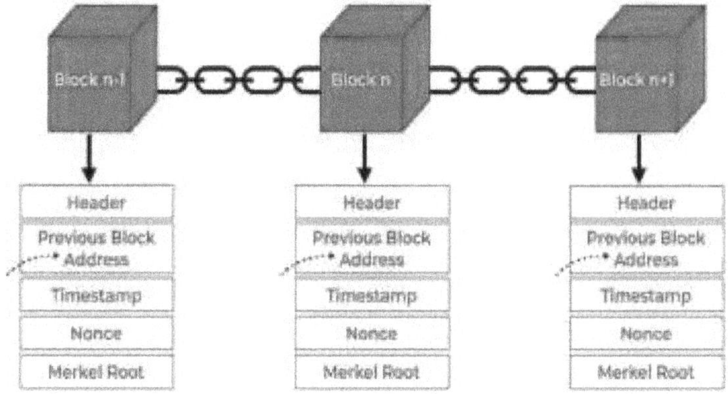

Fig.1.1. Structure of Blockchain

Blockchain is an open, decentralized, distributed, and public digital ledger where transactions are securely recorded across multiple computers (nodes). These nodes are linked through cryptography, forming a growing chain of time-stamped blocks. The fundamental principle of blockchain technology is its capacity to enable secure, direct transactions between parties without the necessity of a third-party intermediary. This decentralized ledger allows all authorized nodes within the network to access the data or records stored on the blockchain. The use of cryptographic techniques to encrypt these records ensures their protection and integrity [2]. As a result, blockchain is an immutable, distributed digital public ledger that may record a variety of data types in addition to financial transactions. Although blockchain is a relatively new technology, it has already had a significant impact across a variety of industries.

The process of a blockchain begins when a transaction is initiated, grouped into a block, and then broadcast to all participating nodes for verification. Each node validates the transaction against a set of predefined rules. Once a majority of the network's participants approve the transaction, the new block is added to the existing chain, and the updated ledger is distributed and stored across all participating nodes, which ensures redundancy and transparency. This peer-to-peer architecture eliminates the need for third-party intermediaries, which streamlines transactions and reduces associated costs.

1.2.1. Features of Blockchain

Blockchain technology exhibits a set of distinctive features that collectively underpin its robustness, security, and applicability across diverse domains. These features distinguish blockchain from conventional centralized systems by ensuring trust in a trust less environment, enabling secure and transparent transactions, and fostering decentralized collaboration. Leveraging foundational properties—specifically decentralization and immutability (see Fig. 1.2)—the framework eliminates single points of failure.

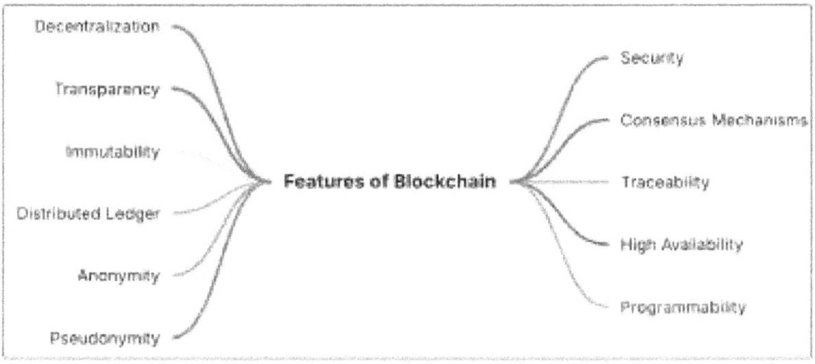

Fig.1.2. Features of Blockchain

smart contracts and consensus mechanisms, blockchain delivers a unique combination of transparency, security, and automation. Additionally, attributes like traceability, high availability, and pseudonymity extend its applicability to areas including finance, supply chain, healthcare, and energy systems. The following table summarizes the principal features of blockchain, along with their definitions, practical examples, and associated benefits, providing a comprehensive understanding of its technological strengths. Table 1.1 shows the key features of blockchain technology.

Table 1.1: Key features of Blockchain

Feature	Definition	Example	Key Benefits
Decentralization	A system design where information is kept and managed across	The Bitcoin network operates without	It gets rid of single points of failure, makes the system stronger,

	various nodes, not depending on a single central authority.	a centralized banking system.	and boosts its ability to handle faults.
Immutability	It makes sure that once data is added to the blockchain, it can't be changed or removed.	Confirmed Bitcoin transactions are irreversible.	Maintains data integrity, prevents tampering, and fosters trust.
Transparency	All participants in the network can see recorded transactions, based on the type of blockchain.	Ethereum's public ledger displays all transaction histories.	Promotes accountability, improves auditability, and strengthens trust.
Security	Employs cryptographic algorithms to secure data and validate transactions.	SHA-256 encryption in Bitcoin transactions.	Safeguards against fraud, unauthorized access, and malicious attacks.
Consensus Mechanisms	Protocols that ensure agreement among distributed nodes before adding new blocks.	Proof of Work (Bitcoin), Proof of Stake (Cardano).	Validates transactions reliably, maintains ledger consistency, and prevents double-spending.
Distributed Ledger	Every participating node keeps a synchronised and identical copy of the ledger.	Every Bitcoin miner keeps a complete copy of the blockchain.	Improves resilience, prevents data loss, and ensures synchronization.

Traceability	Links each transaction to preceding ones, creating a verifiable audit trail.	Hyperledger in supply chain management.	Enhances accountability, enables asset provenance tracking, and supports regulatory compliance.
Programmability (Smart Contracts)	Sets up specific rules that run on their own when certain conditions are satisfied.	Ethereum-based decentralized finance (DeFi) applications.	It cuts down on the need for middlemen, makes sure things run automatically, and helps reduce mistakes made by people.
Anonymity & Pseudonymity	Enables transactions without revealing actual user identities, using cryptographic addresses instead.	Bitcoin wallet addresses mask user identity.	Protects user privacy while maintaining transaction verifiability.
High Availability	Achieved through data replication across nodes, ensuring accessibility even during failures.	Blockchain continues operation despite node outages.	Guarantees continuous service, reduces downtime, and improves reliability.

1.3. Cyber Threat : Challenges and Blockchain Based Solutions

Blockchain technology, while inherently decentralized and immutable, remains susceptible to various cyber threats. A significant example is the fifty one percent attack, where adversaries controlling most of the network computational resources can alter transaction records, compromise system integrity and trust, and causing potential financial losses. Moreover, vulnerabilities in smart contracts, such as coding flaws or loopholes, expose blockchain systems to exploitation, enabling unauthorized fund transfers and other malicious activities, thus underscoring the necessity for stringent security measures during development [5, 6]. In the broader cybersecurity context, Cyber Threat Intelligence (CTI) plays a critical role by employing advanced techniques to identify and analyze current and emerging threats [7, 8]. Effective CTI integration is essential for mitigating risks such as phishing attacks, which deceive users into revealing private keys and enable the theft of digital assets. The rise of Decentralized Finance (DeFi) platforms has further attracted sophisticated cyberattacks, highlighting the need for continuous monitoring, robust security protocols, and resilient blockchain architectures.

According to a recent SANS report [9], CTI priorities include inter-organizational collaboration, selective automation, the evolution of CTI teams, and active information sharing. Complementary research [10] emphasizes the value of frameworks such as STIX, SWRL, OWL, and Dynamic Risk Management (DRM) for improving CTI efficacy, while other studies [11, 12] present security frameworks pertinent to CTI implementation and associated challenges.

1.3.1. Various Cyber Threats and Their Effects

The integrity of the computing environment is under threat from cyber-attacks. Cyberspace, though not real, has become a crucial concept for understanding the dangers posed by advanced weaponry. While some cyber threats may be mere annoyances, others pose significant risks, potentially even life-threatening. A landscape of these cyber threats is illustrated in Fig.1.3 and further elaborated through the following discussion.

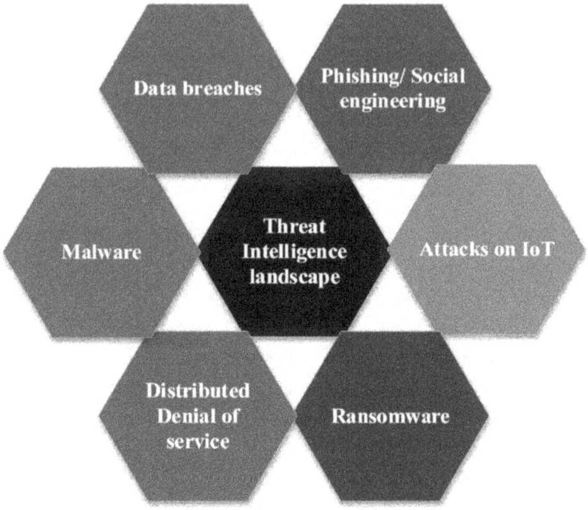

Fig.1.3. Threat Intelligence landscape

Malware: Malware, which stands for "malicious software," is created to break into or damage a computer system. It includes threats like trojans, viruses, and worms, often entering through email attachments, downloads, or system vulnerabilities. Its main functions include stealing, encrypting, or erasing data, hijacking computer functions, or secretly monitoring user activity. Malware spreads through physical media like USB drives and internet downloads.

Ransomware: Ransomware attacks happen when someone encrypts a victims data and then asks for money to give back access. These attacks can range from minor annoyances to severe incidents, often spreading through phishing or infected websites. People in this situation have to make a tough decision between paying the ransom or potentially losing their data forever. The growing threat of ransomware highlights the importance of strong cybersecurity measures.

Social Engineering: Social engineering attacks involve tricking people into revealing sensitive information or accessing systems. These attacks are a major cause of data breaches, as hackers exploit emotions to bypass security protocols. Unlike technical attacks, social engineering relies on psychological manipulation. Preventing these attacks requires strong employee training and awareness.

Phishing: Phishing is when attackers use social engineering to deceive people into giving away sensitive information or downloading malware by sending fake emails or creating misleading websites. It is one of the most common and dangerous cyber threats due to its effectiveness and ease of execution. The widespread use of electronic communication makes phishing a persistent risk, necessitating stringent security measures and employee education.

DDoS: DDoS attacks flood a target's network with too much traffic, leading to interruptions in operations. These attacks vary in complexity and are challenging for businesses and governments. DDoS attacks obscure the distinction between legitimate and malicious traffic, aiming to cause downtime and financial loss. Effective network management is crucial to defending against these attacks.

Man-in-the-Middle Attack: A man-in-the-middle (MitM) attack happens when someone sneaks in and intercepts, and maybe even changes, the communication between two people. Both the sender and receiver are unaware of the intrusion, making this attack particularly dangerous in sensitive contexts like military or financial communications. MitM attacks exploit network vulnerabilities, underscoring the need for robust encryption and authentication measures.

Attacks on IoT Devices: IoT devices, from industrial sensors to consumer gadgets, are increasingly targeted due to their widespread use and outdated security. Hackers can exploit these devices for unauthorized data access or to launch larger attacks like DDoS. The proliferation of connected devices creates numerous opportunities for cybercriminals, making strong security practices and regular updates essential to protect against breaches.

Data Breaches: Data breaches happen when someone gains unauthorised access to sensitive information, which can result in identity theft, damage to reputation, or even surveillance. These breaches can have severe and long-lasting consequences for both individuals and organizations. Hackers exploit system vulnerabilities or human error to gain access to data. Preventing breaches requires a combination of technical safeguards and heightened employee awareness.

In the face of these pervasive threats, it is imperative to develop robust cybersecurity solutions tailored to address each specific challenge. The next section will explore strategies and technologies designed to mitigate the risks associated with these cyber threats.

1.3.2. Standard Cyber Security Frameworks As Solutions

Cyber challenges are really important because they can lead to major issues like power outages, problems with military gear, and leaks of national security information. The impact of cyber-attacks on daily life and critical infrastructure cannot be overstated. To mitigate these risks, individuals and industries can adopt various protective measures. Security experts in the industry have developed and implemented frameworks designed to safeguard systems against cyber threats. These frameworks usually aim to achieve protection goals, like stopping unauthorised access to devices by using controls such as usernames and passwords. The Control Framework helps in creating a fundamental security strategy for the team, offering a foundational set of controls that are prioritised for implementation. Program Frameworks evaluate how a security program is doing, help create thorough security programs, gauge the security of those programs, analyse competitors, and improve communication between security teams and business leaders. Risk frameworks provide important steps for assessing and managing risk. They offer a structured way to handle risk management, which includes identifying, measuring, and prioritising security activities. These frameworks are what industry experts are using right now.

1. The Payment Card Industry Data Security Standard, or PCI DSS, is a set of security guidelines that companies need to follow when they handle branded credit cards from major card networks. Card brands require this and it's regulated by the Payment Card Security Standards Council, which was created to improve the security of cardholder data and help decrease credit card fraud.
2. NIST-CSF: The NIST-CSF is created to safeguard essential infrastructure such as power plants and dams. It features a core framework that outlines cybersecurity roles and processes: identify, protect, detect, respond, and recover.

   The Centre for Internet Security (CIS) provides a scalable model that is really helpful for organisations that are just getting started. It's divided into three categories: basics, foundational, and organisational.

3. The ISO/IEC 27000 series, especially ISO 27001 and 27002, sets international standards for information security. It requires organisations to establish an Information Security Management System (ISMS) that takes into account various challenges and vulnerabilities.
4. HIPAA, or the Health Insurance Portability and Accountability Act, provides a series of regulations and a compliance framework. It also includes enforcement measures like audits of controls, which are somewhat similar to the PCI Security Standards.
5. COBIT is a framework that helps manage IT systems specifically in the area of financial accounting.
6. The General Data Protection Regulation (GDPR) in the European Union establishes strict rules for safeguarding sensitive information, providing clear guidelines while allowing for some flexibility in enforcement.

1.4. Blockchain Consensus Algorithms

In recent years, blockchain technology has become more important, with studies predominantly concentrating on the basic consensus mechanisms. Most current research centres on public blockchain's, utilizing advanced distributed algorithms or existing consensus algorithms. However, on consortium Blockchains, various application scenarios have been developed, yet few researchers have paid attention to custom consistency algorithms. Moreover, building consensus procedures often requires an equilibrium between security and performance. This section presents consensus algorithm which is designed to creating unique security identities for network nodes by segregating voting and bookkeeping rights.

Blockchain technology has revolutionized business and industrial operations by addressing the risks and inefficiencies in business transactions [13–18]. Transaction data pertaining to both tangible and intangible assets is kept in blocks that are sequentially connected to form a chain, acting as a distributed ledger that is shared among network nodes [19, 20]. To ensure immutability and stop the insertion of malicious data, transactions are timestamped, grouped according to block size, and cryptographically linked using the hash of the previous block [21]. Secure, verifiable transactions are made possible without the need for middlemen by each network node updating and storing the entire ledger [22, 23]. Blockchain enables consensus among nodes to validate data, improving integrity and security in contrast to traditional distributed databases that rely on third parties and are subject to delays, increased costs, and security threats [24, 25]. The architecture of how blockchain works is depicted in Fig.1.4.

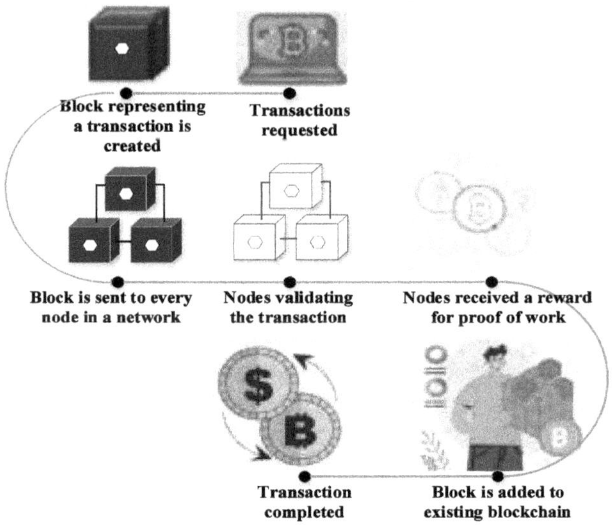

Fig.1.4. Working of Blockchain

1.4.1. Consensus Mechanisms In Blockchain Systems

Consensus mechanisms are the foundational element of any distributed system, particularly blockchain technology, as they provide the means for multiple processes or network nodes to agree on a single, consistent state of data, even in environments prone to faults or malicious activities. Without an effective consensus algorithm, a decentralized ledger cannot maintain data integrity, as disagreements between nodes would lead to inconsistencies and potential vulnerabilities. The selection of a consensus mechanism really affects the security, scalability, performance, and resilience of the blockchain network in significant ways.

Given the diversity of blockchain applications from cryptocurrency networks to critical infrastructure systems there is no universal consensus algorithm that fits all requirements. Instead, designers must make trade-offs between security, performance, decentralization, and energy efficiency based on the intended use case. Consensus mechanisms in blockchain can be grouped into proof-based and vote-based methods, and there are also various hybrid and specialised algorithms that have come up to tackle specific operational issues.

1. Proof-Based Consensus Mechanisms

In proof-based consensus, nodes must demonstrate certain "qualifications" such as computational work, financial stake, or established trust to earn the right to append a new block to the blockchain. These qualifications serve as deterrents to malicious behaviour by making attacks costly or infeasible.

- **Proof of Work (PoW)** - Proof of Work, which gained popularity through Bitcoin, involves miners tackling intricate cryptographic challenges. The first miner who solves the puzzle gets to add the next block and earns a reward in cryptocurrency. Proof of Work provides solid security assurances since an attacker would have to dominate over 50% of the entire network's hash rate to alter the ledger. But it has some downsides, like using a lot of energy, having higher latency, and facing scalability issues because the mining process takes up so many resources.

- **Proof of Stake (PoS)** - Proof of Stake (PoS) substitutes computational work with a system of validation based on stakes, where nodes, known as validators, are selected to generate new blocks according to the quantity of cryptocurrency they secure as collateral. Even though PoS is way better for energy use compared to PoW, it still has some issues like stake centralisation. This happens when rich participants can end up having too much control, which could hurt the whole idea of decentralisation.

- **Proof of Trust (PoT)** - PoT determines validators based on node trustworthiness, often calculated from historical behaviour and reputation metrics. It may incorporate cryptographic techniques like Shamir's Secret Sharing for secure key distribution and RAFT leader election to enhance accountability in systems such as crowdsourcing services. PoT aims to improve reliability by rewarding long-term trustworthy participation.

2. Vote-Based Consensus Mechanisms

In vote-based consensus, nodes explicitly communicate and vote on the validity of new blocks. A block is committed to the chain only after the network reaches agreement, often by achieving a predefined majority or quorum.

- **Practical Byzantine Fault Tolerance (PBFT)** - PBFT is a classical consensus protocol tailored for permissioned blockchains where nodes are known and authenticated. It can tolerate up to (n-1)/3 Byzantine faults, making it resilient to both accidental and malicious failures. However, PBFT suffers from communication overhead that grows quadratically with the number of nodes, limiting scalability in large networks.
- **Proof of Vote (PoV)** - PoV, often applied in consortium blockchains, separates voting rights from bookkeeping rights to enhance security and prevent conflicts of interest. Only core consortium members participate in the voting process, and their decisions determine block creation and validation. PoV offers better efficiency and security compared to PBFT in scenarios where membership is partially trusted, such as energy grid management.
- **Delegated Byzantine Fault Tolerance (DBFT)** - DBFT modifies PBFT by introducing delegated validators (bookkeepers) elected by network participants. This significantly reduces communication complexity, enabling higher throughput and faster finality. DBFT is widely used in blockchain platforms like NEO, where efficiency is a priority.

3. Other Emerging Consensus Algorithms

Beyond the proof-based and vote-based categories, several innovative consensus models have been proposed to improve scalability, throughput, and adaptability:

- ELASTICO – Designed for permission less blockchains, ELASTICO partitions the network into smaller committees that process transactions in parallel, significantly improving throughput while maintaining security.

- Implicit Consensus – Removes global agreement requirements by allowing each node to maintain its own blockchain. Nodes interact opportunistically, achieving unbounded throughput through self-interested validation.
- Ripple Consensus Algorithm – Uses a network of mutually trusted nodes to validate transactions. Periodic rounds of agreement require ≥80% node approval before a transaction is confirmed, enabling faster consensus in partially trusted networks.

1.4.2. Design Considerations and Application to Critical Infrastructure

The selection of an appropriate consensus mechanism is a multi-criteria decision-making process influenced by factors such as:

- Transaction rate and throughput
- Scalability in node participation
- Tolerance to adversarial attacks
- Latency and time-to-finality
- Communication complexity and bandwidth usage
- Energy consumption
- Security against double-spending and history revision

For power grid applications, such as those modelled in the IEEE 118 BUS SYSTEM 118-bus system, the proposed PoV-based consensus offers an optimal balance of performance, fault tolerance, and security, particularly against fifty one percent attacks and other Byzantine behaviours. By leveraging controlled voting rights and consortium governance, PoV addresses the limitations of conventional PBFT and PoW/PoS mechanisms, ensuring that operational data remains both accurate and secure.

1.5. Power Grid System Model

The infrastructure and functioning of power and energy systems have been greatly improved by the integration of cutting-edge protection and control technologies with creative power generation designs. Various protective measures and control techniques are necessary to guarantee the dependability of smart energy systems. The use of digital techniques in power systems has increased significantly in recent decades due to the vital role that energy supplies play in day-to-day living. Advanced tools are increasingly incorporated into modern technologies, such as smart homes, buildings, appliances, and gadgets. Additionally, research in this area has been influenced by recent advancements in communication systems and intelligent security techniques [26, 27]. Fig.1.5 presents the key components in the context of power grids.

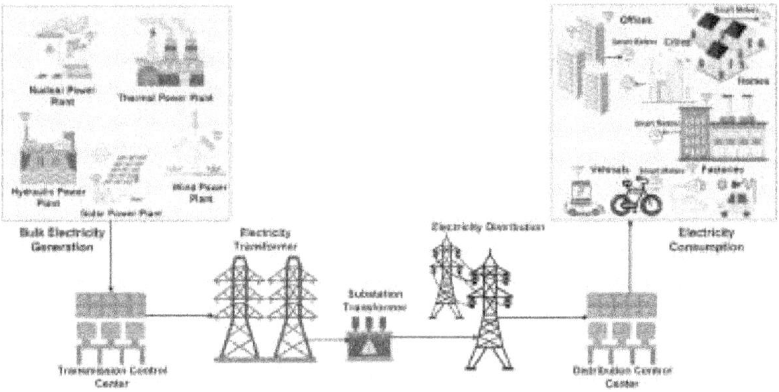

Fig.1.5. Key Components of power grids

1.5.1. Evolution of Power Grids

The adaption from traditional, unidirectional power grids to modern, intelligent power grid architectures represents a critical step towards improving the dependability, effectiveness, and robustness of energy systems. Historically, conventional power grids operated on a centralized generation model, where electricity was produced at large-scale facilities and transmitted in a one-way flow from production to end-users. This architecture lacked real-time monitoring capabilities and exhibited limited adaptability to changing demand or unexpected disruptions, rendering it vulnerable to faults, operational inefficiencies, and emerging cyber threats.

Traditional Power Grids: Legacy power grids are primarily defined by centralized generation, unidirectional energy flow, and minimal real-time control mechanisms. The absence of distributed monitoring infrastructure often results in delayed fault detection and extended recovery times following disruptions. Furthermore, the dependency on a small number of centralized assets creates single points of failure, while the lack of integrated security mechanisms exposes these systems to both physical and cyber vulnerabilities.

Advancement through Technological Integration: To address these inherent limitations, modern power systems incorporate advanced digital technologies that enable bidirectional power flow, decentralized control, this led to real-time decision-making and the development of power grids. Key enabling technologies for this transformation include Supervisory Control and Data Acquisition (SCADA) systems, Wireless Sensor Networks (WSNs), and Phasor Measurement Units (PMUs).

SCADA: SCADA forms the backbone of operational monitoring and control in advanced power grids. It enables operators to remotely supervise and manage critical infrastructure components, such as substations, transformers, and circuit breakers. SCADA systems collect diverse operational data including voltage, current, breaker status, and frequency from multiple points across the grid, while also issuing control commands to optimize performance and respond to anomalies. These systems provide real-time situational awareness, enabling rapid identification and mitigation of faults. However, traditional SCADA architectures were not inherently designed to address modern cybersecurity risks, leaving their communication channels susceptible to intrusion, interception, or manipulation by adversaries.

WSNs: WSNs enhance the data acquisition capabilities of power grids by deploying spatially distributed autonomous sensors to monitor environmental and electrical parameters, such as temperature, voltage, current, and moisture. The collected data is cooperatively transmitted to central systems for analysis. Within a power grid context, WSNs enable fine-grained, real-time monitoring from geographically dispersed locations, including smart meters at consumer premises. This granular visibility facilitates advanced applications such as demand-side management, predictive maintenance, and automated fault detection, thus improving both operational efficiency and resilience.

PMUs: PMUs represent an advancement in power system monitoring, offering high-speed, time-synchronized measurements of electrical waveforms (phasors) across wide geographic areas. By leveraging Global Positioning System (GPS) signals for precise synchronization, PMUs enable operators to assess the dynamic state of the power grid with unprecedented accuracy. This capability allows for the early detection of subtle oscillations, stability issues, or abnormal patterns that could indicate equipment malfunction or a potential cyberattack. Despite their benefits, PMUs introduce potential vulnerabilities, particularly in scenarios where GPS signals are disrupted or spoofed, compromising data integrity.

1.5.2. Impact of Integration on Power Grid Performance

The convergence of SCADA, WSN, and PMU technologies has transformed the power grid into a smart, responsive, and adaptable system. This integration supports advanced operational capabilities, including:

- Monitoring grid assets in real-time and controlling them in a decentralised way.
- Automated fault detection, isolation, and system self-healing.
- Effortless combination of distributed energy resources and renewable energy sources.
- Enhanced energy efficiency, operational reliability, and situational awareness.

However, while these technologies provide transformative benefits, their interconnected nature significantly expands the cyberattack surface. The communication networks that interlink SCADA, WSN, and PMU components are particularly vulnerable, as successful exploitation could allow adversaries to disrupt operations, manipulate data, or compromise decision-making processes. Therefore, securing these effective communication channels are crucial for ensuring the stability and reliability of next-generation power grids.

1.6. Design Model Of Blockchain

Blockchain, initially developed for cryptocurrency networks like Bitcoin [28], offers a decentralized, cryptographically secured method for storing historical data, account records, and other information within a peer-to-peer distributed network [29]. Data is stored in linked blocks, each containing a hash of the previous block, ensuring chronological integrity [30]. Any attempt to alter data would require recalculating the compromised block and all subsequent ones, making manipulation computationally infeasible. This security is reinforced by blockchain consensus mechanisms, peer-to-peer transmission, distributed storage, and cryptography [31]. There are different types of blockchains, including public, private, and consortium ones [32]. Public blockchains, while open, face regulatory restrictions due to limited controllability. Consortium blockchains offer partial decentralization, combining the benefits of public and private systems, and have gained traction in sectors like banking, exemplified by the R3 CEV project [33]. Technology eliminates the need for trusted intermediaries in online transactions, reducing risks like identity theft and platform failures [34].

BFT based consensus, including PBFT and BFT-SMART [35, 36], relies on majority voting, enhancing efficiency but reducing safety due to fewer nodes. PoV [37, 38], a variant tailored for consortium blockchains, separates voting and bookkeeping rights, enabling improved throughput and reduced communication complexity, especially with large node counts. Blockchain's immutability and security make it promising for power grid cybersecurity. Despite research interest, comprehensive analysis from application and technical perspectives remains limited. Key security considerations include fifty one percent attack tolerance, resistance to manipulation, and finality trade-offs [39], motivating novel approaches for improved grid protection.

1.6.1. Blockchain-Based Cybersecurity Enhancement for Advanced Power Grids

The integration of advanced monitoring and control technologies such as SCADA systems, WSNs, and PMUs has transformed conventional power grids into power grids. This transformation has brought substantial benefits, including real-time monitoring, improved efficiency, and automated fault detection. However, it has also introduced increased susceptibility to sophisticated cyberattacks, particularly targeting the communication channels that interconnect these systems. In this context, blockchain technology appears to be a potential solution for enhancing the security of essential power grid infrastructure and addressing threats like the fifty-one percent attack.

1.6.2. Addressing SCADA Communication Channel Vulnerabilities

SCADA systems plays a central role in modern power grid management by enabling remote monitoring and control of critical infrastructure. Nevertheless, traditional SCADA architectures often rely on centralized control models and proprietary communication protocols, which were designed before the emergence of contemporary cyber threats. Consequently, SCADA communication channels remain vulnerable to multiple types of attacks:

- Man-in-the-Middle (MITM) Attacks – Adversaries intercept and modify control commands or sensor data, potentially causing unsafe operational decisions.
- False Data Injection (FDI) Attacks – Malicious data is deliberately inserted into the communication stream, misleading operators and automated decision-making systems.
- Denial-of-Service (DoS) Attacks – Communication channels are flooded with excessive requests, causing operational delays or outages.

Blockchain technology provides a decentralised and unchangeable system that tackles these weaknesses by removing dependence on a single control point and maintaining data integrity.

1.6.3. Blockchain-Enabled Secure SCADA Communication

A blockchain-based approach to securing SCADA communication channels can be implemented through the following mechanisms:

- **Secure Data Transmission and Storage**: Every node in the power grid system, whether it's a smart meter at a user's home, a sensor in a substation, or a PMU, can have its own unique public-private key pair assigned to it. Before sending, the gathered data gets encrypted with some really advanced cryptographic methods, like the Whirlpool hash algorithm for creating message digests and the Schnorr digital signature scheme for authentication. This makes sure that the data being sent is kept private and stays accurate. After verification, this data gets logged on the blockchain ledger, forming a permanent and tamper-proof record.
- **Tamper-Proof Data Records**: The structure of blockchain is designed to be unchangeable, meaning that when a data block is added to the ledger, trying to alter it would involve recalculating the hash values for that block and every block that comes after it, which is really difficult to do. This ensures that the operational data sent through SCADA communication channels keeps its integrity and authenticity during its entire lifecycle.

- **Decentralized Verification:** Blockchain uses a distributed verification process instead of depending on a central authority for data validation. Every authorised node could access, verify, and update the ledger using a peer-to-peer consensus mechanism. This decentralised method really makes it harder for an attack to succeed if it starts from just one compromised control centre.

1.6.4. Mitigating the fifty one percent Attack in Power Grids

In blockchain networks, the fifty one percent attack refers to the scenario where an adversary gains control over the majority of the network's computational or consensus power, enabling manipulation of the transaction history. In a power grid context, such an attack could enable the falsification of operational data or issuance of fraudulent control commands. A robust blockchain consensus mechanism is critical for mitigating this threat.

Proof of Vote (PoV) and Extended Proof of Vote (EPoV) - Unlike PoW, which is computationally expensive and energy-intensive, PoV employs a voting-based mechanism among trusted consortium members such as authorized utility operators, substations, and authenticated smart meters. Voting rights (decision-making authority) are distinct from bookkeeping rights (ledger maintenance authority), reducing the risk of collusion or monopolization of control. Only authenticated nodes with verified identities participate in voting, increasing security against node impersonation or Sybil attacks. EPoV enhances PoV by optimizing voting efficiency and integrating advanced cryptographic protocols, further reducing latency while maintaining security guarantees.

Decentralized Arbitration and Attack Resilience - Under the PoV/EPoV model, consensus is achieved through distributed arbitration, wherein a block's validity is determined by the voting results of multiple geographically and organizationally diverse nodes. Even if an attacker compromises a subset of nodes, they must still control a majority of voting power to execute a fifty one percent attack a significantly more challenging requirement in a well-structured consortium blockchain. The immutable and transparent nature of blockchain records guarantees that any malicious activity, regardless of its temporary success, generates a verifiable forensic trail. This facilitates post-attack analysis, recovery, and system improvement.

From Perimeter Defence to Intrinsic Security - Traditional power grid cybersecurity strategies have often relied on perimeter defence protecting the boundaries of the network from intrusion. While useful, this approach becomes less effective against insider threats or distributed attacks. By embedding blockchain-based consensus mechanisms directly into the communication and control fabric of the power grid, security shifts from an external barrier to an intrinsic property of the network.

Through decentralized validation, immutable data storage, and strong cryptographic protection, blockchain technology particularly when paired with PoV/EPoV provides a robust security architecture capable of countering advanced cyber threats, including the fifty one percent attack. This approach enhances both the reliability and resilience of modern power grids, ensuring secure, transparent, and tamper-proof operations.

1.6.5. Distributed Blockchain Framework for Power Grid Cybersecurity

In todays landscape, cybersecurity is a critical concern for both industries and the academic sector, driving the adoption of various monitoring and defence techniques to bolster the resilience of modern SG technologies. The vulnerability of power grids to cyber threats has been exacerbated by their growing dependence on digital systems, such as fifty one percent attacks that can undermine data integrity and system control. To address the challenges, a cybersecurity management system leveraging a distributed blockchain-based approach needs to be developed. This harnesses the power of the larger community to identify and mitigate vulnerabilities, ensuring resilient and secure operations within power grids by preventing malicious actors from gaining majority control over the network.

1.6.6 Role of Blockchain technology in securing grid operations

Electricity underpins modern civilization and economic growth, yet many global power grids are outdated, relying on one-way transfer processes for production, transportation, and distribution [40]. These systems are vulnerable to cyber threats [41], highlighting the need for more reliable and resilient solutions. The U.S. Energy Independence and Security Act of 2007 introduced the concept of a SG an advanced energy infrastructure that integrates digital management, monitoring, and self-healing capabilities, improving efficiency, reliability, and reducing carbon footprints by incorporating renewable energy sources [42].

Power grids are rapidly evolving with the help of WSN and IoT [43-45]. The IoT enables communication between intelligent devices, optimizing energy use and allowing consumers to become producers, or "prosumers" [46-49]. However, this interconnectedness also increases vulnerability to cyberattacks such as man-in-the-middle attacks, DoS, and false data injection [50]. Distributed blockchain technology, which connects IoT devices through a network of SDN controllers, offers a robust solution by ensuring secure data transmission and storage [51, 52]. Even with improvements such as phasor measurement units (PMUs), existing systems are still vulnerable to attacks because they depend on GPS [53, 54], emphasizing the need for enhanced security measures [55-57].

Blockchain technology, initially introduced by Satoshi Nakamoto [61], provides a decentralized, tamper-resistant ledger, eliminating the importance of getting validation from an outside source. This technology is used in many different fields, like finance, healthcare, and transportation [58-64]. In power grids, blockchain can facilitate peer-to-peer transactions and data distribution, enhance system reliability and preventing single points of failure [65]. The decentralised nature of blockchain helps keep data integrity, confidentiality, and availability intact, making it a promising option for securing power grid operations from fifty-one percent attacks [66-68].

1.7. Fifty-One Percent Attack

Blockchain technology has become a game-changer for securing data transmission, storage, and operational control in different fields, including essential infrastructure like smart power grids. However, despite its promise of decentralization and immutability, blockchain is not inherently immune to certain classes of attacks. Among these, the fifty one percent attack also known as the majority attack is considered one of the most important challenges, especially for blockchain networks that rely on PoW consensus mechanisms. In the context of a blockchain-secured smart grid, this vulnerability poses not only economic risks but also potential threats to public safety and national security.

1.7.1. Definition and Operational Mechanism of the fifty one percent Attack

When a single malicious entity or a coordinated group acquires control over more than half of the network's total mining or processing power, a fifty one percent attack occurs. This majority control grants the attacker the ability to subvert the normal consensus process, allowing them to rewrite transaction histories and override the honest majority's operations. In a PoW blockchain, miners are in a race to solve cryptographic puzzles. This process helps validate transactions and add new blocks to the ledger. The network follows the longest chain rule states that the chain with the highest total computational work is considered the valid chain. An attacker with more than 50% computational power gains the ability to:

- **Accelerate Block Mining:** Generate valid blocks faster than the rest of the network, effectively dominating block creation.
- **Transaction Censorship:** Prevent legitimate transactions from being included in blocks.
- **Double Spending:** Reverse their own transactions after they have been confirmed, enabling fraudulent reuse of the same digital assets.
- **Monopolization of Block Production:** Ensure that only their blocks are added to the blockchain, sidelining honest participants.

1.7.2. Consequences for Public Blockchain Networks

While the fifty one percent attack is theoretically possible on any PoW network, the feasibility depends on the network's total computational capacity. Large-scale networks like Bitcoin require immense hashing power to achieve such control, rendering the attack highly resource intensive. Conversely, smaller, less distributed blockchain systems such as those in early deployment phases are more susceptible due to lower aggregate computational requirements. The integration of blockchain into power grid operations is intended to enhance data integrity, decentralize control, and secure operational commands. However, the occurrence of a fifty one percent attack in this environment could lead to severe disruptions, including:

- **Manipulated Meter Data:** An attacker could falsify critical operational parameters, such as power generation levels, consumption data, and system load profiles. This could cause billing errors, misallocation of resources, or destabilization of grid operations.
- **Fraudulent Control Commands:** Maliciously validated commands could trigger deliberate outages, overload specific network segments, or manipulate renewable energy dispatch, leading to:

- Localized or widespread blackouts.
- Physical damage to grid infrastructure.
- Disruption of energy trading and market settlements.

- **Consensus Corruption on Grid State:** The blockchain's purpose as a tamper-proof ledger of grid activity would be undermined, leading to conflicting records of the operational state and complicating recovery efforts.
- **Data Censorship and Information Leakage:** Selective blocking or alteration of alerts and sensor data could blind operators to real-time threats or anomalies.

1.7.3. Proposed Mitigation: Extended Proof of Vote (EPoV) Consensus

To address this vulnerability, the proposed Extended Proof of Vote (EPoV) consensus mechanism introduces two critical innovations:

- **Separation of Voting and Bookkeeping Rights:** By decoupling the rights to validate transactions from the rights to maintain ledger records, EPoV reduces the risk that majority ledger control translates into consensus dominance.
- **Decentralized Voting among Verified Consortium Members:** EPoV relies on a permissioned voting structure, where only authenticated meter nodes and utility stakeholders participate in consensus. This significantly increases the difficulty of coordinating a fifty one percent attack, as it would require both computational and organizational compromise.

The voting-based structure ensures that the acceptance or rejection of blocks depends on collective agreement among trusted participants rather than raw computational dominance. As a result, even if some nodes are compromised, the chances of a successful fifty-one percent attack are significantly lowered.

While blockchain offers promising advancements in securing smart grid communication and control systems, vulnerabilities like the fifty one percent attack must be explicitly addressed in the design of consensus mechanisms. The EPoV approach, by incorporating identity-based voting rights and separating them from bookkeeping authority, transforms the attack feasibility from a purely computational challenge into a complex organizational and security problem. This not only mitigates the immediate threat of majority attacks but also enhances the overall resilience of blockchain-based power grid infrastructures.

1.7.4. Fifty one percent attack and its implications

The integrity of computing environments, particularly those underpinning critical infrastructures such as power grids, is increasingly challenged by sophisticated cyberattacks. Although blockchain technology offers significant security advantages through its decentralized architecture and immutable ledger, it is not entirely immune to exploitation. One of the most severe vulnerabilities affecting certain blockchain networks is the fifty one percent attack, a malevolent entity or consortia gets control of more than half of the network's entire processing power (hash rate).

Fig.1.6 shows how the fifty one percent attack happens. This majority control enables the attacker to manipulate the consensus mechanism, with potentially severe consequences:

1. Disruption of Transaction Confirmation
   - By controlling the consensus process, attackers can intentionally delay or entirely block the validation of new transactions.
   - This interference leads to network congestion, degraded performance, and reduced reliability, undermining trust in the blockchain's operational integrity.
2. Double-Spending Attacks
   - The attacker can reverse previously confirmed transactions, effectively enabling the same cryptocurrency or digital asset to be spent multiple times.
   - Such fraudulent actions directly cause financial losses and erode confidence in the network's ability to guarantee transaction finality.
3. Modification of Blockchain History
   - Although blockchain records are cryptographically linked, a fifty one percent attacker can generate a longer alternative chain, replacing the honest chain with a manipulated one.
   - This control allows the attacker to redefine the blockchain's historical record, effectively dictating what is considered the "truth" within the network.

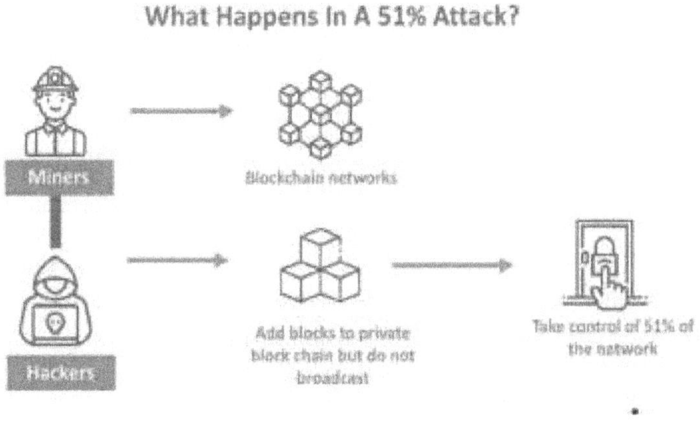

Fig.1.6: Process Flow of a fifty one percent Attack in Blockchain

In the context of power grids where blockchain may secure operational data, control signals, or transaction records, a fifty one percent attack can result in catastrophic outcomes. Imagine an attacker gaining control over most meter nodes in a power grid system; they could then:

Injection of False Data - Maliciously altering meter readings or operational commands could destabilize grid operations, cause incorrect load balancing, or even trigger large-scale blackouts.

Blocking of Legitimate Control Commands - By intercepting or rejecting valid operational instructions, attackers can disrupt electricity distribution, delay emergency responses, or impair restoration efforts following an outage.

Alteration of Operational History - By rewriting the historical record of grid operations, attackers can prevent accurate post-incident analysis, hinder forensic investigations, and obstruct effective recovery.

The combination of decentralized control systems and critical infrastructure dependencies means that a fifty one percent attack on blockchain-based power grid applications is not merely a financial threat, but a national security risk. This underscores the necessity for robust consensus algorithms, anomaly detection mechanisms, and multi-layered security architectures to safeguard blockchain deployments in such environments.

1.8. Motivation For Research

Prior research indicates that employing a PoV consensus mechanism in blockchain technology could significantly enhance data security within contemporary power grid systems. Previous studies have identified vulnerabilities, specifically the risk of fifty one percent attacks, in the integration of blockchain and power grid technologies. We have thoroughly evaluated the system's performance concerning potential attacks and have found it to be effective in mitigating these threats. Consequently, utilising smart meters as components in a distributed network, where the data from the meters is organised into blocks, aims to enhance the resilience and security of the power grid infrastructure. Using PoV in our suggested distributed blockchain framework not only improves security but also strengthens resistance to cyber-attacks. Looking ahead, future work will focus on fortifying protections against cyber threats while balancing the need for privacy and regulatory compliance. This aim will enhance the functionality of our blockchain system utilizing the PoV consensus. Specifically, we are concentrating on the Extended PoV approach to better safeguard personal information while ensuring confidentiality.

1.9. Problem Statements

Vulnerability to fifty one percent Attacks - Despite blockchain's inherent security features, existing implementations in smart grid systems remain susceptible to fifty one percent attacks, leading to data manipulation and system-level compromise.

Lack of Tailored Consensus Mechanisms - Conventional consensus algorithms like Proof of Work (PoW) or Proof of Stake (PoS) are computationally intensive and unsuitable for energy-constrained devices like smart meters, necessitating a lightweight and secure alternative such as Proof of Vote (PoV).

Limited Integration of Smart Meters as Blockchain Nodes - There is a gap in practical frameworks that integrate smart meters as active blockchain nodes, capable of both validating and storing encrypted energy usage data in a secure and scalable manner.

Trade-Off Between Security and Privacy in Power grids - Current blockchain-based energy systems struggle to balance robust security mechanisms with the preservation of user privacy and compliance with data protection regulations.

Insufficient Defence Against Data Injection and Cyber Threats - Existing distributed energy network architectures lack sufficient protection against false data injection attacks (FDIAs) and targeted cyber intrusions, especially in decentralized scenarios.

Inadequate Support for Real-Time Monitoring and Decision-Making - Blockchain systems in power grids often suffer from latency and throughput issues, hindering their effectiveness in real-time monitoring, consensus, and fault response.

Underdeveloped Frameworks for Extended PoV Implementation - There is limited research on adapting and extending the Proof of Vote consensus model for high-security, privacy-preserving, and regulatory-compliant power grid environments.

1.10. Objective of Research

Objective 1 - ***To propose an Extended-PoV Consensus Algorithm to attain resilience and consistency of the communication channel.***

This objective focuses on designing an advanced consensus mechanism—Extended-Proof of Vote (EPoV)—that builds upon traditional PoV to enhance the reliability and consistency of communication in blockchain-based power grid systems. The EPoV algorithm aims to address limitations in existing consensus methods like PoW and PBFT by offering reduced latency, higher throughput, and improved fault tolerance. The emphasis is on making the communication channel between power grid components more robust and less prone to disruption, ensuring seamless operation even under cyber threat conditions.

Objective 2 - ***To create sturdier blockchain, using WhirlSchnorr: A Hybrid Cryptographic Scheme to reconfigure SCADA.***

This goal centers on increasing the security and structural integrity of blockchain systems used in industrial control environments, particularly Supervisory Control and Data Acquisition (SCADA) systems. By incorporating Whirlpool Hash Algorithm (WHA) for efficient and secure data compression and Schnorr signatures for robust cryptographic authentication, the blockchain network becomes more tamper-resistant and verifiable. The enhanced cryptographic approach aims to reconfigure traditional SCADA infrastructures to withstand sophisticated cyberattacks and unauthorized intrusions.

Objective 3- ***To design and implement proposed blockchain framework using Extended-PoV to improve resilience in power grids communication channel, IEEE 118 BUS SYSTEM-118 Bus system is used for simulation.***

This objective involves the practical realization of the theoretical framework, where the EPoV-based blockchain is implemented and evaluated within a simulated power grid environment. The IEEE 118 BUS SYSTEM-118 Bus system is used for performance validation, offering a realistic and complex testbed to assess communication resilience, fault tolerance, latency, and scalability. The framework aims to prove its effectiveness in mitigating cyber threats and improving real-time operational efficiency in large-scale power grid networks.

1.11. Proposed System Overview

Hyperledger Fabric, a private permissioned blockchain, has been added to a layered power grid system in Fig.1.7 to make it better. It starts by generating electricity, just like in real life, and then it transmits and distributes energy. Smart meters and other devices provide you particular information about how you use them. Blockchain nodes check and monitor the system utilising SCADA, PMUs, and WSN modules.

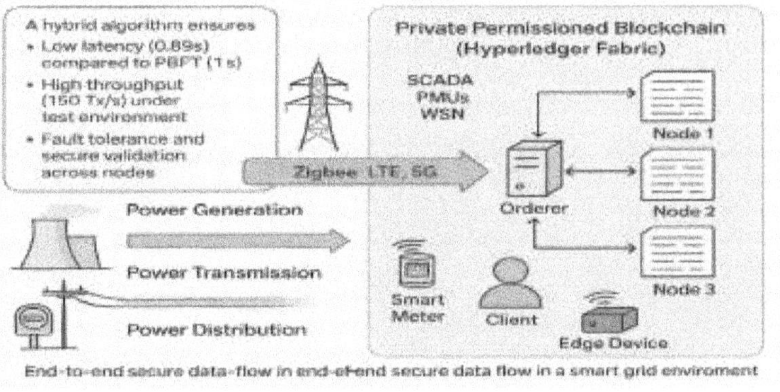

Fig.1.7: Proposed Blockchain Framework

A combined algorithm (Whirl-Schnoor + E-POV) makes sure that everyone agrees and that problems are handled. An Ordered, Nodes 1, 2, and 3 keep track of transactions in the blockchain architecture. Nodes get data from clients and devices that has been checked, which increases confidence in the network. Data communication is easier with ZigBee, LTE, and 5G. The total system has a latency of 0.89 seconds and a speed of 150 Tx/s. This integration makes sure that data may be sent safely between power grid endpoints. This makes it possible to build energy infrastructure that can grow.

1.12. Major Contribution Of The Thesis

Development of a Novel EPoV-Based Framework: Proposed a blockchain-based architecture integrating Extended Proof of Vote (EPoV) consensus tailored to smart power grids, specifically designed to mitigate fifty one percent attacks and enhance network integrity.

Lightweight and Scalable Security Layer: Designed a lightweight and scalable solution suitable for real-time deployment in distributed power grid environments, addressing the challenges of latency and processing overhead in traditional blockchain models.

Integration of Whirlpool Cryptography: Introduced Whirlpool hashing in place of conventional SHA mechanisms, improving collision resistance and overall cryptographic robustness within the power grid data chain.

Smart Meter Node Architecture: Utilized smart meters as blockchain nodes, encoding meter readings as secure transaction blocks to ensure data authenticity, immutability, and decentralization in the energy ecosystem.

Enhanced Privacy and Confidentiality Mechanisms: Proposed an Extended PoV approach to balance data privacy and regulatory compliance, protecting personal information while maintaining transparency in grid operations.

Comprehensive Evaluation and Simulation: Conducted detailed performance evaluation and attack simulations, validating the proposed system's effectiveness against cyber-attacks, consensus failures, and communication delays.

1.13. Novelty

- The proposed framework is the **first of its kind to combine Extended Proof of Vote (EPoV)** with modern cryptographic methods specifically for **mitigating fifty one percent attacks in power grids**.
- Unlike traditional models, the framework is **lightweight, fast, and scalable**, making it practical for **real-time deployment** in critical infrastructure.
- **Threat intelligence mechanisms** empower the system to autonomously adapt to emerging threats and abnormal patterns.
- The system functions as a **fully decentralized security layer**, eliminating single points of failure and improving interoperability across multiple grid networks.
- Utilization of **Whirlpool hashing** provides a highly secure alternative to SHA-based mechanisms, reducing the risk of collision attacks.

Scope of the research –

This research looks at how to design, develop, and evaluate a blockchain-based framework that uses Extended Proof of Vote (EPoV) consensus and modern cryptographic techniques. The goal is to improve the security and resilience of smart power grids against fifty-one percent attacks. The proposed system is designed to create a lightweight, scalable, and real-time deployable solution that fits well in critical infrastructure environments.

The research encompasses the implementation of Whirlpool hashing for improved data integrity and resistance to collision attacks, and the development of threat intelligence modules capable of detecting and responding to abnormal behaviours autonomously. Additionally, the framework promotes full decentralization, eliminating central points of failure while enabling interoperability across heterogeneous grid systems.

Performance metrics such as latency, consensus time, computational overhead, and threat mitigation accuracy will be studied through simulation and experimental validation. The scope also includes evaluating the feasibility of integrating smart meters as blockchain nodes and testing system robustness under various adversarial conditions.

Overall, the research is directed toward enhancing the security, efficiency, and adaptability of blockchain-enabled energy systems using novel consensus and cryptographic strategies.

1.14. Organization of Thesis

This thesis is organized in **eight structured chapters**, each addressing a distinct facet of the research while maintaining a coherent progression from fundamental concepts to advanced frameworks, experimental validation, and concluding insights. The arrangement ensures that the reader is guided through the intellectual journey of problem identification, literature survey, innovative solution design, performance evaluation, and future research directions.

Chapter 1 – Introduction

This chapter lays the conceptual groundwork for the study by **establishing the significance of cybersecurity in critical infrastructure systems**, with an emphasis on modern power grids. It articulates the growing complexity of cyber threats in the energy sector, the vulnerabilities arising from increased digitization, and the limitations of existing defence system. The chapter also presents the **motivation** for employing blockchain technology as a robust, transparent, and decentralized security enabler. Key elements include the **problem statement**, **precisely defined research objectives**, **scope of work**, and the **expected contributions** of the thesis. This foundation not only contextualizes the study but also highlights its novelty and societal relevance.

Chapter 2 – Literature Survey

This chapter delivers a **comprehensive and critical review** of existing work on blockchain technology, exploring its fundamental properties such as decentralization, immutability, and consensus-driven validation. It assesses blockchain's applicability to cybersecurity in distributed infrastructures, **with a special focus on the resilience it offers against targeted cyber intrusions**. Key blockchain frameworks, consensus algorithms (like Proof of Work, Proof of Stake, and voting-based systems), and application-specific adaptations are examined in depth. Moreover, it identifies **research gaps**—particularly the limitations in scalability, latency, and resistance to advanced cyber threats—thereby justifying the research direction undertaken in this thesis.

Chapter 3 – Extented Proof-Of-Vote (E-Pov) Consensus Mechanism For Cyber-Resilient Power Grid Frameworks

This chapter introduces the **Extended Proof of Vote (E-PoV)** consensus mechanism, a novel consensus protocol tailored to improve the security and operational efficiency of power grid networks that use blockchain technology. The chapter offers a **rigorous theoretical exposition** of E-PoV, detailing its architecture, communication flow, and cryptographic safeguards. The **attack resilience model** is elaborated, showing how E-PoV mitigates various threat vectors, including coordinated cyber-attacks, data tampering, and network partitioning. Simulation results and analytical performance comparisons with conventional consensus mechanisms substantiate its effectiveness, highlighting **improvements in consensus finality, fault tolerance, and resource efficiency**.

Chapter 4 – Distributed Blockchain Framework for Fifty-One Percent Attack Protection in Power Grids

This chapter presents a **specialized distributed blockchain-based defence architecture** aimed at neutralizing the notorious **fifty-one percent attack**—a critical vulnerability in public and consortium blockchain deployments. The design emphasizes **node decentralization, dynamic validator selection, and adaptive difficulty adjustment** to minimize the likelihood of a malicious majority takeover. Detailed technical schematics illustrate the interaction between system components, consensus logic, and verification nodes. The framework's **robustness is validated** through adversarial modelling and stress-testing, demonstrating its capacity to maintain network integrity under extreme attack scenarios.

Chapter 5 – Blockchain-Enabled Cyber Defense In Modern Power Systems: The Grid-Lock Approach

This chapter introduces the **Grid-Lock Secure-Chain** framework, an **integrated blockchain consensus model** designed to protect against multi-vector cyber threats, including **zero-day exploits, data poisoning, and synchronized distributed attacks**. The framework's architecture combines **layered cryptographic defence, proactive threat detection, and consensus-level anomaly handling**. Real-world case studies and simulated threat models demonstrate its ability to **pre-empt, contain, and recover from cyber incidents** while ensuring minimal disruption to critical grid operations.

Chapter 6 – Result and Discussion

This chapter synthesizes the **experimental and simulation-based evaluation** of all proposed frameworks and consensus models. The discussion integrates **comparative performance analysis** across parameters such as transaction throughput, latency, energy efficiency, scalability, and attack resistance. Results are interpreted against the backdrop of research objectives, providing a **balanced assessment** of each method's strengths, limitations, and potential deployment trade-offs. Special attention is given to **inter-framework synergy**, where hybridizing certain design elements may yield further performance enhancements.

Chapter 7 – Summary, Conclusion, and Future Work

This chapter provides a **holistic summary of the research contributions**, distilling the essential outcomes from each preceding chapter. It reaffirms how the proposed solutions address the research objectives and **advance the state of the art in blockchain-enabled cybersecurity for power grids**. Limitations encountered during the study are openly discussed, providing transparency for future researchers. Finally, **strategic future directions** are proposed, such as integrating **quantum-resistant cryptographic primitives**, enhancing **interoperability in grid monitoring systems**, and leveraging **threat modelling** for proactive defence.

Chapter 8 – References

This chapter compiles a **comprehensive, meticulously formatted bibliography** covering blockchain fundamentals, consensus mechanisms, cryptographic advancements, power grid security strategies, and distributed system architectures. The references ensure scholarly rigor and traceability of all concepts, methodologies, and comparative benchmarks presented in the thesis.

1.15. Summary

The introduction of this thesis provides a comprehensive examination of blockchain technology, highlighting its core advantages such as decentralization, immutability, and security. It delves into the potential of integrating blockchain, emphasizing how this combination can enhance decision-making and data protection across various sectors. The discussion extends to the realm of cyber threat intelligence, outlining the challenges faced by modern systems and presenting blockchain-based solutions as effective countermeasures. The thesis also addresses various cyber threats, particularly those targeting power grids, and explores the mechanisms for attack detection and prevention. One important area of study is blockchain consensus algorithms, which are essential for ensuring the integrity and reliability of data in these systems. The introduction further examines the use of blockchain technology in designing power grids involves proposing a distributed blockchain framework that focusses on improving cybersecurity in power grid operations. Finally, it underscores the important role of blockchain in securing power grids, ensuring resilient and reliable energy infrastructure in the face of evolving cyber threats.

1.16. Conclusion

This work demonstrates that blockchain technology provides a strong and practical framework for enhancing the cybersecurity of critical infrastructures such as power grids. By leveraging its inherent properties of decentralization, immutability, and transparency, blockchain addresses key vulnerabilities, ensuring data integrity and preventing unauthorized access. The integration of consensus algorithms further safeguards against threats such as fifty-one percent attacks, preserving the integrity and reliability of grid operations.

The findings highlight that distributed blockchain frameworks can significantly improve the security, resilience, and operational continuity of power grids. As energy systems transition toward smarter, more interconnected architectures, blockchain emerges as a critical enabler of future-proof, resilient infrastructure. This research highlights how blockchain-based solutions can strengthen power grid security against changing cyber threats, leading to dependable and continuous energy services.

CHAPTER 2

LITERATURE SURVEY

2.1. Introduction

This section explores the existing literature on blockchain security, emphasizing the study of various consensus algorithms and their applications within blockchain technology. It examines how these consensuses mechanisms help improve the overall security and efficiency of blockchain systems, highlighting both their assets and weaknesses. In addition, the section offers a perspective on the changing landscape of blockchain security, discussing emerging trends and potential areas for future research. First, this paper discusses how blockchain is utilized across multiple domains through its integration with AI, highlighting the advantages and key characteristics of each referenced study. Following this, the survey reviews existing literature on various consensus algorithms and their applications within blockchain technology. Next, it examines the security architecture of blockchain in power grid applications, as proposed by various authors. Finally, the paper explores how distributed blockchain solutions are employed to counter cyber threats on power grids, summarizing the contributions of different researchers.

2.2. Survey on Blockchain Integration across Multiple Domains

The potential of this disruptive technology to generate significant advancements is demonstrated by Casino et al [69] in their comprehensive analysis of the application of blockchain technology across multiple domains when integrated with AI. The investigation not only emphasises the transformative influence of blockchain but also explores the precise characteristics that render it a potent innovation instrument. The research also provides a comprehensive classification of blockchain applications in a variety of sectors, such as healthcare, banking, finance, and supply chain management, to demonstrate the diverse ways in which this technology is transforming traditional industries.

Mufti et al. [70] provide the most recent trends and major advancements in blockchain technology, focussing on the finance and banking industries. This study highlights how blockchain technology is transforming various industries by improving security and operational efficiency.

Another assessment by Ekramifard et al [71] examined the advantages of combining blockchain and AI in real-time applications. They claim that this combination considerably improves the security, efficiency, and productivity of a variety of applications.

Also, JD Harris and others suggested a framework where participants can work together to create datasets and use smart contracts to keep the structure updated all the time. This framework works really well in situations where a model is used over and over again for similar inputs, like in personal assistance systems or recommendation engines. The research indicates that working together in this way can result in more precise and adaptable models, which could enhance the integration of AI and blockchain in practical uses.

Marwala and Xing [73], Sung-Bong [74], and Zheng [75] each offer a detailed examination of how combining blockchain and AI could influence the future of technology. This convergence is highlighted as the next big step in technology, with the ability to change many industries by improving automation, security, and decision-making. Research indicates that as blockchain and AI technologies develop, using them together will lead to the next wave of innovation in fields like finance, healthcare, and smart systems.

Researchers such as V. M. Ambika et al [76], B. Aruna et al [77], Sri PSGA et al [78], A. Yashaswini et al [79], and Bhargava et al [80] concentrate on tackling security challenges associated with blockchain and AI. The articles look at different ways to tackle these challenges, offering useful insights for creating more secure systems. These studies are really important for pushing research forward in the field. They set the stage for future innovations that could help reduce security risks tied to new technologies.

Pratuisha et al [81] and Sahu and Swain [82] introduced a proposed system that uses artificial neural network techniques for estimating coronary artery disease, which is really important for healthcare. Their research shows how AI can improve diagnostic accuracy and lead to better patient outcomes. In a similar way, [83] introduce a better data hiding technique that utilises bit differencing and LSB matching, while also providing a thorough analysis of an improved artificial bee colony optimisation method for addressing economic load dispatch issues. These contributions show how AI and optimisation techniques can be used in many different areas, like healthcare and energy management.

Researchers such as Ragavan et al [84], Behera and Gangopadhyay [85], Pravin et al [86], Elavarasan et al [87], Talaat et al [88], and Priyadharsini et al [89] suggest new approaches to improve data security by integrating cryptography with different artificial intelligence algorithms. Their work is all about making network systems more secure, coming up with new ways to keep sensitive data safe from possible threats. These reviews together provide a detailed look at the future possibilities in these areas, pointing out parts that need more investigation. We also put together some important characteristics in Table 2.1 to help give more insights into the current research and what it might mean for the future.

Table 2.1. Existing studies with their key findings

Authors	Proposed Solution	Key Features	Limitations
Casino et al [69]	Systematic review of blockchain applications	Comprehensive classification: identification of trends and use cases	Lacks domain-specific depth; limited empirical evidence
Gorkhali et al	Overview of blockchain evolution and literature	Covers various platforms; historical and architectural insights	No structured taxonomy; generic discussion
Taylor et al	Review of blockchain for cybersecurity	Security-centric analysis; addresses attack vectors	Limited coverage of non-security aspects
Ekramifard et al [70]	Blockchain-AI integration review	Focuses on technical overlap between AI & blockchain	Needs real-world implementation examples

Harris et al [71]	Decentralized AI systems using blockchain	Empirical cases; focus on collaborative intelligence	Scalability issues not fully addressed
Marwala et al [72]	AI-enhanced blockchain systems	Theoretical integration models; potential use cases	Conceptual in nature; no performance evaluation
Sung-Bong et al [73]	Survey of blockchain use cases	Broad domain applications; analytical approach	High-level overview; lacks performance benchmarks
Zheng et al [74]	Blockchain intelligence systems	Explores AI-enhanced blockchain decision-making	Trade-off between complexity and speed not discussed
Salah et al [75]	Challenges in blockchain for AI	Identifies research gaps and security challenges	Lacks practical deployment insights
Jaoude et al [76]	Blockchain adoption across domains	Domain-specific examples; empirical data	Not AI-focused
Pandl et al [77]	AI and blockchain convergence review	Future research roadmap; framework identification	Overlaps in categorization; no empirical validation
Hughes et al [78]	Blockchain research landscape	Benefits, risks, policy suggestions	Broad scope with minimal technical depth
Goyal et al [79]	Blockchain for decentralized social media	Focus on content control and trust	Specific to social platforms; not generalizable

Sgantzos et al [80]	AI implementations on blockchain	Real-world use cases; emerging trends	Scattered findings; lacks unified architecture
Rath et al [81]	Challenges in blockchain with emerging AI technologies	Technology mapping; integration trends	Focuses more on challenges than solutions
Sharma et al [82]	Conceptual integration of AI and blockchain	Theoretical synergy model; use case hints	No empirical data or implementation
Queiroz et al [83]	Blockchain in supply chain management	Domain-specific review; logistics and traceability	Limited AI relevance
Khezr et al [84]	Blockchain in healthcare systems	Patient data security; smart contracts	Privacy regulation challenges; technical overhead
Kaur et al [85]	AI transformation in banking	Customer personalization; fraud detection	Specific to finance; less focus on blockchain
Siyal et al [86]	Blockchain in medicine	Medical record handling; security & transparency	Requires further standardization
Gurtu et al [87]	Literature review on blockchain in SCM	Decentralized trust in supply chains	Implementation challenges in legacy systems
Labazova et al [88]	Taxonomy of blockchain applications	Classification by maturity & domain	Hype vs reality contrast not validated with field studies
Dinh et al [89]	Integration model of AI and blockchain	Disruptive innovation model; proposes synergy layers	Real-time processing and scalability remain bottlenecks

Hamsa Gayatri et al	IoT, AI, and Blockchain convergence	Edge data handling; smart environment enablement	Integration complexity; limited deployment case studies

2.3. Survey on Consensus Algorithms in Blockchain Technology

Luu et al. [90] proposed ELASTICO, a scalable consensus algorithm designed specifically for permissionless blockchains. ELASTICO addresses the computational intensity of the mining process by partitioning the blockchain system into smaller, manageable units called committees. This partitioning allows for parallel processing, where each committee handles a different subset of transactions, thereby increasing the overall transaction rate in direct proportion to the computational resources available. The algorithm is resilient, capable of withstanding adversarial attacks even when an opponent controls up to 25% of the system's computational power. The key innovation in ELASTICO lies in its probabilistic approach to agreement, which distinguishes it from traditional Byzantine consensus algorithms. Each committee within the system employs Byzantine consensus to verify the accuracy of transactions against a defined constraint function. Only transactions that satisfy this function are accepted. The final consensus is achieved by aggregating the inputs from all committees, ensuring robustness and security.

In other studies, Luu et al [91] introduced SCP, which is a Byzantine-based consensus algorithm that is computationally scalable and designed for blockchain systems. SCP stands out because it can adjust how much bandwidth it uses, mainly by changing things like the difficulty of Proof of Work (PoW). The scalability of the algorithm means it can boost throughput as computational power improves, which makes it a good fit for different processing power levels among miners. SCP spreads out the network by evenly distributing transactions across data blocks, which means there's no need for a central certificate and it reduces the risk of a single point of failure. The algorithm uses a Merkle tree structure to stop double spending, making sure that each transaction output is checked locally.

Borran et al. [92] explored the Byzantine consensus problem in asynchronous systems, especially in cases where these systems move towards partial synchrony. Creating a leaderless, deterministic algorithm for these systems is really complicated because it's tough to keep everyone on the same page without having a central leader. The study suggests a method that extends leaderless consensus from synchronous systems to semi-synchronous ones without the need for a leader. The process includes all nodes talking to each other in rounds to come to an agreement, using a technique based on the interactive consistency problem that is usually found in synchronous systems. The algorithm brings in two new features: a parameterised consensus process that can handle disagreements according to different fault models, and robust validation to improve the accuracy of consensus.

Gervais et al. [93] did a quantitative analysis to look into the security and effectiveness of Proof-of-Work (PoW) blockchain networks, paying attention to different network and consensus-related features. PoW is commonly found in current blockchain systems, but there hasn't been much focus on its security evaluation in the literature. The research used a simulator to investigate how blockchain performance relates to security, especially looking at how variations in block size and block interval affect selfish mining and double spending. The results indicate that larger block rewards make double spending attacks less likely, and keeping a block size of 1 MB with a 1-minute interval doesn't weaken security.

Porat et al. [94] conducted a detailed analysis of the Proof-of-Work (PoW) consensus algorithm, exploring its effects on blockchain implementations. When the algorithm gets harder, it takes more time to mine extra blocks, which results in more invalid blocks and longer forks. The study goes over different uses of blockchain technology, especially highlighting the Nakamoto consensus mechanism that Bitcoin relies on. This process includes nodes working on a cryptographic puzzle to create new blocks, where the first node to discover a solution essentially wins a "lottery" and shares the block with the network. The idea is that no one node has more than 50% of the network's processing power, which helps keep things secure.

Abraham et al. [95] looked into how Byzantine Fault Tolerance (BFT) algorithms can be used in blockchain systems, examining the technology through a layered approach. This study looks at a solution that brings together the Nakamoto algorithm and BFT, trying to merge the benefits of both methods to improve consensus and security in blockchain networks.

Crain et al. [96] suggested a consensus method for consortium blockchains that eliminates the requirement for signatures, leaders, or randomness. This method makes the complex multivalued Byzantine consensus problem easier by turning it into a binary one. It allows for consensus to be reached in a constant time frame when binary instances are run at the same time. The design is shown to be the most efficient choice for consortium blockchains, offering a strong solution for reaching consensus.

Ren et al. [97] proposed an implicit consensus architecture where each node manages its own blockchain, enabling unlimited throughput. This setup swaps out the BFT termination property for a self-interested one, resulting in linear message complexity. This approach has a unique feature where it introduces checkpoint blocks that don't need consensus, unlike transaction blocks. This study looks at the theory behind how this architecture performs and the various factors that affect it.

Garcia and others [98] looked into how Proof-of-Stake (PoS) consensus algorithms are put into practice in blockchain systems. Proof-of-Stake (PoS) is different from Proof-of-Work (PoW) because it doesn't need a lot of computational power to solve cryptographic puzzles. Instead, PoS chooses block signers based on how much cryptocurrency each node holds, which helps to lower energy consumption. The study goes over protocols like Ouroboros and Casper, which use PoS with methods like secure coin-flipping and time slot synchronisation to choose stakeholders and keep the network secure.

King and others introduced PPCoin, which is a peer-to-peer cryptocurrency that uses a Proof-of-Stake (PoS) algorithm aimed at lowering energy consumption while maintaining network security. The PoS approach takes into account "coin age," meaning how long a currency has been held, when choosing who gets to create blocks. This is different from the competitive race seen in PoW systems. This approach makes it easier to understand double spending attacks, as it needs a certain amount of currency to create a fake block in the blockchain.

Zou et al. [100] introduced the Proof-of-Trust (PoT) consensus algorithm aimed at enhancing accountability in crowdsourcing services. This algorithm figures out who the transaction validators are by looking at node trust and uses Shamir's secret-sharing method along with the RAFT leader election process. The approach tackles the scalability problems of traditional Byzantine Fault Tolerance (BFT) by breaking the consensus process down into four distinct phases. The initial stage is all about electing an RAFT leader within the consortium, and then the voters will choose the transaction validators. During the third phase, a selected group of nodes is responsible for validating transactions, and in the final phase, these validated transactions are incorporated into the blockchain. The algorithm is really good at managing node failures, making sure that the number of nodes involved in the consensus process matches the number of Byzantine nodes.

Jeon et al. [101] presented the Randomised Mesh Blockchain (RMBC), which utilises a DBFT (Delegated Byzantine Fault Tolerance) consensus algorithm to address the shortcomings of Proof-of-Work (PoW) and conventional BFT algorithms. RMBC has a two-step consensus process. In the first step, it uses the BFT algorithm to reach an initial agreement. Then, in the second step, it brings together relevant departments, and a verifier from each department checks the transactions. This two-step process is designed to stop invalid transactions, even when there are more bad actors around.

Fu and colleagues [102] created the Proof of Participation and Fees (PoPF) consensus algorithm for JCLedger, which is a blockchain solution part of the JointCloud framework. JointCloud lets developers tailor cloud services, and JCLedger employs PoPF to reach consensus while using very little computational power. Mining candidates are chosen according to the fees they pay and how often they participate as accountants. The study includes experimental analysis and simulation to look at how accountants are distributed, but it doesn't really dive into the accuracy and performance of the algorithm.

Schwartz and others [103] explained Ripple as a consensus algorithm that uses subnetworks that are mutually trusted. Ripple works in a circular way, where nodes regularly come to an agreement on a list of transactions that are considered valid. The process includes gathering candidate sets, voting on whether transactions are valid, and needing at least 80% of nodes to agree on a transaction before it gets added to the ledger. Ripple works to make sure that every node has the same up-to-date version of the latest closed ledger, which helps avoid forks and keeps the network consistent.

Li et al. [104] introduced the Proof of Vote (PoV) consensus algorithm, which aims to be a more energy-efficient option compared to PoW. In a consortium blockchain, PoV employs a voting mechanism that involves various roles such as commissioner, butler candidate, butler, and regular user, all of whom take part in the validation process. The algorithm shows much lower power consumption than PoW, which makes it a good choice for high-performance blockchain networks. Nakamoto et al. [105] came up with the Proof of Work (PoW) consensus algorithm, where miners race to solve complicated mathematical puzzles, and the first one to crack the puzzle gets a reward. The challenge level of these puzzles matches the overall computational strength of the network, which helps maintain a consistent rate of block mining. Even though it's commonly used, PoW gets a lot of criticism for needing a lot of computing power and taking a long time to process. Table 2.2 presents the current studies along with their characteristics.

Table 2.2. Existing studies with their key findings

Authors	Algorithm Name	Proposed Solution	Key Features	Limitations
Luu et al. [90]	ELASTICO	Sharded blockchain with parallel committee processing	Partitioned committees; Probabilistic Byzantine Consensus; high throughput	Limited to 25% adversarial resilience; requires trusted randomness
Luu et al. [91]	SCP	Scalable Byzantine consensus protocol	PoW difficulty adjusts bandwidth;	May suffer from high bandwidth

			Merkle tree to avoid double spending	under certain conditions
Borran et al. [92]	–	Leaderless deterministic consensus model	Interactive consistency; fault-tolerant; no single leader	Performance under partial synchrony not fully evaluated
Gervais et al. [93]	PoW Blockchain Security	Performance/security modelling of PoW blockchains	Analysis of block rewards and difficulty; double-spending mitigation	High resource usage remains unresolved
Porat et al. [94]	Proof-of-Work Analysis	Analytical study on PoW trade-offs	Nakamoto Consensus; insight into forks and difficulty correlation	More forks under high difficulty levels
Abraham et al. [95]	–	Hybrid model combining BFT and Nakamoto consensus	High-security integration; enhanced consensus	Still computationally intensive
Crain et al. [96]	–	Binary Byzantine consensus for consortium networks	Efficient binary consensus; multi-valued	Tailored for consortiums; may not scale to public networks

			transformatio n	
Ren et al. [97]	Implicit Consensus	Nodes run independent chains with checkpointing	Unbounded throughput; decentralized checkpoint validation	Complexity in checkpoint consistency
Garcia et al. [98]	Proof-of-Stake (PoS)	Energy-efficient alternative to PoW	Protocols like Ouroboros and Casper; reduced energy consumption	Requires initial wealth distribution; staking centralization risk
King et al. [99]	PPCoin	Coin age-based PoS consensus	Low energy requirement; age-weighted block selection	Susceptible to nothing-at-stake and simplified double-spending
Zou et al. [100]	Proof-of-Trust (PoT)	Trust-based consensus for crowdsourcing	RAFT + **Shamir's** Secret Sharing; node reliability-based validators	Needs precise trust evaluation; complexity in trust model
Jeon et al. [101]	RMBC with DBFT	Randomized mesh blockchain with dual-stage consensus	BFT phase + department verifier; mesh topology	Design complexity; practical implementatio n challenges

Fu et al. [102]	Proof of Participation and Fees	Consensus with minimal computation in JointCloud	Fee-based and participation-frequency-based selection	Security analysis not detailed
Schwartz et al. [103]	Ripple	Circular protocol among trusted subnetworks	Requires 80% node agreement; voting-based transaction validation	Only works in partially trusted settings
Li et al. [104]	Proof of Vote (PoV)	Lightweight voting-based consensus in consortium chains	Voting by commissioner, butler, and peers; low power	Depends on governance structure; not suitable for permissionless settings
Nakamoto et al. [105]	Proof of Work (PoW)	Classic puzzle-solving mining with incentives	Adjustable difficulty; mining rewards; robust under open networks	High energy cost; long confirmation time

The current research on blockchain consensus algorithms has some significant gaps, especially when it comes to assessing the speed and security of the proposed algorithms. When looking at blockchain consensus solutions, it's super important to carefully consider both performance and security. However, a lot of studies don't really cover these factors in depth, usually just giving qualitative comparisons and missing out on quantitative performance metrics. Also, evaluations often miss out on some of the current consensus methods, which makes it tough to figure out how mature a solution really is. This paper looks at important factors for evaluating how efficient and secure different consensus methods are, providing a thorough comparison of new algorithms that have been proposed recently. The insights shared will assist developers in choosing the best algorithm for their blockchain applications and emphasise the importance of further research on consensus methods.

2.4. Survey on Distributed Blockchain Framework For Resilience Against Cyber Threats On Power Grids

Line et al. [114] introduced a security architecture utilizing blockchain for power grid applications. However, the system faces challenges due to the lack of standardization in certain layers of the stack, particularly in cross-protocol areas such as the service layer and the performance monitoring layer, which can impact the issuance and maintenance of security tokens.

Anusha Vangala et al. [115] proposed an innovative power grid-based blockchain-envisioned authenticated key agreement technique tailored for smart farming environments. Compared to other authentication systems, the proposed SCBAS-SF demonstrates superior security at a lower communication cost and offers comparable computational efficiency. Blockchain technology is increasingly recognized as a promising solution for addressing cybersecurity challenges in power grids [115-118].

Sengan et al. [119] looked into how false data cyber-attacks affect the physical layers of power grids. The research looked at using an agent-based method to decentralise how data integrity is protected in the network. The proposed modelling strategies were tested and compared to the current framework-supervised deep learning models to see how efficient and effective they are.

Guan et al. [120] developed a practical yet confidential data aggregation method that prioritizes both security and privacy in distributed systems. In their approach, consumers are grouped into organizations, with each organization maintaining its own private blockchain to securely store the data of its users. To enhance privacy, the authors employed pseudonyms to obscure users' true identities, allowing each user to create multiple pseudonyms and associate their personal information with different pseudonyms, thus ensuring that no single identity is linked to all the data.

This method not only protects the individuals' privacy within each organization but also provides a robust way to manage personal information across various transactions. Additionally, the use of Bloom filters facilitates fast and efficient verification processes, enabling the system to quickly check for the presence of specific data while maintaining the confidentiality of the information. By combining pseudonyms and Bloom filtering, the this approach effectively balances privacy, security, and system performance, providing a scalable solution for privacy-preserving data aggregation.

Liang et al. [121] proposed a decentralised blockchain-based data security architecture to improve the data security of current energy systems against cyberattacks. The suggested architecture takes advantage of the distributed and unchangeable characteristics of blockchain technology, which was initially created to secure digital transactions in Bitcoin cryptocurrency, to safeguard essential energy infrastructure. Decentralising how system data is controlled and stored really boosts the self-defence abilities of power systems, helping them become tougher against possible cyber threats. Blockchain technology makes sure that any changes to system data are logged in a permanent ledger, which offers great security and transparency. This new way of looking at cybersecurity helps us keep an eye on system operations in real-time and makes it easier to spot and react to threats quickly. As a result, the suggested blockchain-based architecture shows a major improvement in protecting today's power grids, providing a strong solution to the increasing threat of cyberattacks aimed at essential energy infrastructure.

A. S. Musleh et al. [122] did a detailed study on how Blockchain technology can be applied in smart grids, looking into various possible implementations and methods for incorporating Blockchain into smart grid systems. Their work explores the design and architecture of Blockchain-based intelligent grid applications, offering detailed insights into how Blockchain can improve the efficiency and security of smart grid operations. Their analysis covers different use cases, including how to improve data integrity, facilitate secure peer-to-peer energy trading, and better manage distributed energy resources. The authors look into the many advantages that Blockchain can offer to smart grids, such as decentralisation, transparency, and resistance to cyber threats, all of which are essential for today's power grid systems. Additionally, their research points out the major technological hurdles related to implementing Blockchain in SGs, including scalability, interoperability, and energy consumption. This study is a helpful addition to understanding how Blockchain can be used in Power grids and highlights the main challenges that need to be tackled for successful implementation.

Wang et al. [123] came up with a decentralised platform for aggregating meter data that focusses on privacy and security. They combined blockchain technology with homomorphic encryption to make it more secure and private. This system uses a hierarchical blockchain framework to collect and verify meter data, utilising a consensus mechanism that is supported by a Byzantine Fault Tolerance (BFT) process. This makes sure that even if there are faulty or malicious nodes, the platform can keep its integrity and keep working as it should. The platform takes advantage of blockchain's distributed nature to make meter data aggregation more resilient and cost-effective. This approach lessens the dependence on centralised systems and boosts scalability.

To address man-in-the-middle threats and file manipulation, including blockchain-based information provenance, Kamal et al. [124] proposed a robust security solution. The method relies on creating link fingerprints using the Received Signal Strength Indicator (RSSI), which are then combined with a pseudo-random nonce to enhance the security of Advanced Metering Infrastructure (AMI). This approach helps in detecting unauthorized access or tampering by calculating statistical values, such as the mean and variance of RSSI readings from connected static smart meters, rather than relying solely on binary values. By utilizing these calculated values, the system can effectively identify malicious nodes and any discrepancies in meter readings caused by tampering. Additionally, the technique ensures that even If someone tries to intercept the communication, they won't be able to easily change the data without getting caught, as the system continuously checks the consistency of the RSSI values across the network. This makes the approach resilient against common attacks such as data injection or replay attacks. The integration of RSSI-based fingerprints with blockchain enhances data provenance, ensuring that any alteration or unauthorized manipulation of data is traceable and verifiable. Overall, Kamal et al.'s method significantly strengthens the security of AMI systems, providing a scalable and effective solution for protecting power grid infrastructure from cyber threats.

Blockchain-based intelligent grid information aggregation and regulation mechanisms were developed by a consortium led by Fan et al. [125]. The Blockchain consortium utilizes a signcryption method that facilitates multidimensional data acquisition and supports communication among multiple recipients. During the regulation process, fixed-height blocks are transmitted from the blockchain to the control center, grid controller, and equipment provider, who decode them to retrieve the plaintext. This mechanism allows each transmitter to perform a multidimensional analysis of the data and generate control plans tailored to specific clients. Grid operators leverage the feedback provided by smart contracts to integrate customer voltage regulation, thereby enhancing the grid's overall efficiency and responsiveness.

Along with the improvements in power grid technology, Blockchain technology has also shown important real-world uses in many areas, such as digital currencies, international payment and settlement systems, supply chain financing, and securities issuance and exchanges.

Jogunola et al. [126] showed how Blockchain can be used for energy peer-to-peer (P2P) trading in the context of the power grid. A smart contract was created and deployed on the IBM platform using Hyperledger Composer in their study to manage trust and payments in the energy P2P trade system. This example shows how Blockchain can make energy transactions between consumers and providers easier and more secure, leading to better trading of energy. The authors talk about some challenges faced when using Blockchain for secure energy P2P trading, like problems with scalability, transaction speed, and handling vulnerabilities in smart contracts. We need to tackle these challenges to unlock the full potential of Blockchain in the energy sector and make sure its integration into power grid systems is secure and efficient.

Liu et al. [127] proposed a Blockchain-enabled solution for the smart power trading mechanism in power grids (SG) that improves the trading process using cellular networks. This system uses wireless communication to gather power information, which is subsequently stored on the blockchain. This information helps smart contracts figure out fair trade terms by making sure that energy transactions are transparent and fair. The design features a dual-chain topology that includes a local blockchain and a renewable energy trading blockchain, which helps make energy exchanges more efficient and flexible. Integrating renewable energy sources makes the system better at energy trading and helps support sustainable energy practices more effectively. The authors also suggested a system that uses Blockchain to provide incentives for renewable energy, aiming to improve the reliability and scalability of renewable energy producers and encourage more involvement from decentralised energy producers. This system boosts energy efficiency and also strengthens grid stability, which makes it a really promising option for future energy markets.

Aybar-Meja et al. [128] introduced a process for integrating Blockchain into a controlled power market. Their method focuses on enhancing transparency and security in power market transactions by utilizing smart contracts and Blockchain technology to verify transactions and enforce rules in real time. The authors emphasized that Blockchain's decentralized nature removes the need for intermediaries, which reduces both transaction costs and the risk of fraud. By creating an immutable and transparent ledger, Blockchain can facilitate secure and efficient trading in controlled power markets, particularly in scenarios where multiple market participants are involved. The integration of smart contracts ensures that energy trades are executed automatically under predefined conditions, further streamlining the process. This approach could prove essential in future power markets that require high levels of regulation and oversight.

Wang et al. [129] came up with a mutual authentication system for power grids (SG) that is secure and efficient. The new system based on Blockchain tackles the ongoing issue of centralised registration certificates, which have been susceptible to different security breaches. By decentralizing the authentication process, this system enhances both the security and efficiency of SG communication. The authors explored several innovative techniques, including batching validation and dynamic Join-and-Exit methods, which optimize the system's performance by reducing communication overhead. Additionally, the security and efficiency requirements for smart meter (SM) identification were evaluated, highlighting the critical role of Blockchain in ensuring secure data transmission. The system enables secure mutual authentication between SMs and utility companies (UCs) with just one round of communication, minimizing delays and improving system performance.

Singh et al. [130] presented a deep learning and homomorphic encryption-based data-gathering method aimed at mitigating the negative effects of flash load on forecasting performance in power grids. Their method applies deep learning algorithms to enhance the precision of load forecasts, and homomorphic encryption keeps the collected data safe and private. This combination helps to lessen the effects of sudden load changes and makes sure that the forecasting process stays efficient and reliable. This encryption method lets us work with and analyse data without needing to decrypt it, which helps keep sensitive information private. By using this secure data aggregation method, Singh et al. created a low-cost, high-performance solution for power grid forecasting that balances security with computational efficiency, making it a suitable option for practical deployment in power grid environments.

You et al. [131] proposed an efficient and resilient Blockchain-based information aggregation strategy that eliminates the need for a trusted authority. The method utilizes the Chinese Remainder Theorem to achieve multidimensional data aggregation, ensuring data privacy and integrity without relying on a centralized entity. This approach supports flexible and dynamic user management, making it adaptable to changing network conditions and user requirements. The system is designed to be fault-tolerant, ensuring that the information aggregation process remains reliable even in the presence of network failures or malicious attacks. By incorporating Blockchain, You et al. enhanced the security and resilience of the aggregation process, making it a robust solution for large-scale and decentralized systems. This methodology promises to play a crucial role in future decentralized applications where trust and reliability are key concerns.

The study [132] looks into open-source multi-agent system frameworks, especially the Python-based framework for heterogeneous agent communities (PEAK), which is intended for modelling power grids. This framework enables real-time integration at pilot locations and supports simulation environments, facilitating detailed analysis and experimentation. The authors present an innovative agent ecosystem built on communities of agents, emphasizing its potential for data analytics and AI-driven models. The PEAK framework is tested in various applications, demonstrating its versatility and effectiveness in power grid scenarios. In a separate study [133], a new tool utilizing Jupyter Notebook and the Python programming language is introduced to create attack graphs for power grids. The tool analyses system design, identifies vulnerabilities, and examines potential attack scenarios. By employing counterexamples, it automatically detects attack sequences, builds corresponding counterexamples, encrypts them for further relaxation, and continues the process until all possible attack sequences are revealed. Table 2.3 shows the existing studies with their key findings along with limitations.

Table 2.3. Existing studies with their key findings

Authors	**Proposed solution**	**Key features**	**Limitations**
Line et al [114]	Security architecture using blockchain for power grid applications	Blockchain technology to secure power grids, addresses security token issuance and maintenance	Lack of standardization in service layer and performance monitoring, impacting cross-protocol interoperability
Anusha Vangala et al [115]	Blockchain-based authenticated key agreement technique for smart farming	SCBAS-SF provides superior security, lower communication cost, and comparable computational efficiency.	Limited application scope (smart farming) and challenges in scalability to broader power grid systems

Sengan et al [119]	Agent-based approach for data integrity protection in power grids against false data cyber-attacks.	Decentralized protection using agent-based approach, compared with supervised DL models.	May not be effective against highly sophisticated cyber-attacks.
Guan et al [120]	Data aggregation method prioritizing security and privacy using pseudonyms and Bloom filters.	Grouping consumers into organizations, private blockchain for secure data storage, pseudonyms to enhance privacy, fast verification.	Complexity in pseudonym management and potential scalability issues.
Liang et al [121]	Decentralized blockchain-based architecture for power grid data security.	Distributed, immutable blockchain ledger to protect against cyber-attacks, real-time monitoring and validation.	Requires high computational resources and may not be suitable for all grid types.
Musleh et al [122]	Blockchain in power grids for data integrity, peer-to-peer energy trading, and resource management.	Focuses on decentralization, transparency, and resilience against cyber threats, with detailed analysis of implementation.	Challenges in scalability, interoperability, and energy consumption.
Wang et al [123]	Blockchain-based privacy-preserving platform for meter data aggregation using	Uses BFT and homomorphic encryption for privacy and security.	Potential computational overhead in real-time applications and compatibility with

	homomorphic encryption.		existing meter systems.
Kamal et al [124]	RSSI-based fingerprinting for AMI systems to prevent tampering and data manipulation.	Combines RSSI-based link fingerprints with pseudo-random nonces to secure AMI systems, detecting tampering and unauthorized access.	May require continuous network monitoring and could be impacted by environmental factors like signal interference.
Fan et al [125]	Blockchain consortium for power grid data aggregation and regulation.	Supports multidimensional data acquisition, smart contract feedback, and communication among multiple recipients.	Complexity in implementing a consortium model and ensuring privacy across various parties.
Jogunola et al [126]	Blockchain for peer-to-peer energy trading in power grids.	IBM Hyperledger Composer for managing trust and payments, aims to improve energy trade security and efficiency.	Scalability issues and transaction speed concerns in large-scale energy trading systems.
Liu et al [127]	Blockchain-enabled smart power trading mechanism using wireless communication.	Dual-chain topology, integrates renewable energy sources and incentivizes decentralized energy producers.	Difficulty in integrating with existing energy systems and regulatory frameworks.
Aybar-Meja et al [128]	Blockchain integration into controlled power markets for enhancing	Smart contracts, decentralized authentication, and real-time transaction verification.	Potential issues in integrating Blockchain into highly regulated power markets.

	transparency and security.		
Wang et al [129]	Blockchain-based mutual authentication system for power grids.	Decentralized authentication, batch validation, and dynamic join-and-exit methods for smart meter identification.	Vulnerabilities in handling large numbers of smart meters in highly dynamic environments.
Singh et al [130]	DL and homomorphic encryption for power grid data gathering to mitigate flash load effects.	Uses DL for forecasting, homomorphic encryption for secure data aggregation.	Computationally intensive, may be difficult to implement in real-time systems.
You et al [131]	Blockchain-based information aggregation strategy eliminating trusted authority.	Multidimensional aggregation using the Chinese Remainder Theorem, ensuring data privacy and integrity without centralization.	Scalability concerns in large decentralized systems, may require robust fault-tolerance mechanisms.

The current research introduces a novel approach to enhancing the security of modern power systems by utilizing advanced distributed security concepts. However, there are potential limitations. The previously proposed frameworks rely on widely distributed geographical sensors, which lead to the creation of numerous communication channels, thereby increasing the complexity of cyberattacks attempting to deceive detection systems into reaching a false consensus. Despite this, both system administrators and cyber attackers have access to technological advancements, such as processing power, communication capabilities, and blockchain technology. Consequently, it is plausible for cyber attackers to exploit these resources. Additionally, cyber attackers could deploy malicious cyber-tampering strategies and virus propagation techniques within decentralized systems and AMI networks, potentially compromising the proposed Blockchain-based security architecture. Thus, the scenario presents a challenge where both attackers and system operators leverage emerging technologies, applying sophisticated security measures and assault strategies.

2.5. Survey Based On Cyber Threat Defense in Power Grids

Ghiasi et al. [134] used the Hilbert-Huang Transform methodology in conjunction with blockchain-based ledger technology to improve signal retrieval and voltage/current signal evaluation in smart sensors and controllers. This technique improves the security framework in power grids by effectively detecting fake data injection attacks (FDIAs), maintaining the grid's integrity and resilience. The methodology uses cosine similarity to identify communities within the power grids, which is crucial for analysing and reducing the effects of harmful activity. However, depending on cosine similarity presents issues, as flaws in community detection may lead to incorrect conclusions, jeopardising the system's stability and dependability during intrusions. Such weaknesses underscore the need for additional advances in community detection algorithms to improve the robustness and resilience of power grids.

Zhong et al. [135] presented a novel distributed authentication and authorisation (A&A) protocol for power grid networks that uses blockchain technology to combat emerging risks. The protocol combines a unique blockchain framework with the immutable ledger and decentralised authentication features of blockchain architectures, making it ideal for power grid systems that require resource access control and identity verification. By examining the security and threat models of earlier A&A protocols, the study established the usefulness of the new protocol in mitigating such attacks. The deployment method employs the FISCO consortium platform and smart contract algorithms to provide a viable implementation of the A&A protocol. While the incorporation of blockchain, decentralised authorisation, and enhanced encryption improves security, it also increases computational complexity and resource needs, potentially slowing down real-time processes and reducing system efficiency.

Jha et al. [136] came up with a blockchain-based synchrophasor communication system aimed at protecting the integrity and security of synchrophasor data. The system is designed to improve the reliability and safety of synchrophasor measurements by using a distributed, decentralised, and hierarchical PDC architecture. The design of this blockchain network, which operates on a peer-to-peer (P2P) basis, takes advantage of the strengths of distributed systems, making it more resilient. Also, the time it takes to mine goes down when there are more miners involved. However, because the consensus mechanism depends on the difficulty level, there's a trade-off between cutting down mining time and having a lot of miners involved.

Mahmud et al. [137] suggested a consensus-based distributed control strategy for managing distributed energy resources (DERs). They used blockchain as a secure way to exchange information, which helps improve cyber resilience. This method meets global control goals by linking each distributed energy resource to a local blockchain server that uses distributed ledger technology, allowing for accurate power sharing between resources and coordinated grid-forming abilities. The system lets nearby assets safely share local measurements, which helps promote teamwork and strengthen resilience. The stability analysis using the Lyapunov function showed that the distributed control stays stable, even when there are changes in communication latency due to blockchain. But, depending on consensus-based blockchain control can cause some delays and add extra computational demands, which might weaken the system's ability to handle cyberattacks and result in slower responses and operational issues.

Liu and colleagues [138] put forward a blockchain-based secure energy trading solution for power grids, which is integrated with wireless networks. The system uses power data gathered through wireless networks and saved on the blockchain, allowing smart contracts to make better trading decisions. A dual-chain setup, which includes a local energy trade blockchain and a renewable energy trading blockchain, enhances the efficiency of power trading and boosts the use of renewable energy. A blockchain-enabled incentive system was proposed to improve the stability and scalability of renewable energy providers. But, adding renewable energy sources and electric vehicles to this trading system makes things more complicated and increases the number of transactions. This could slow things down and make it harder to manage energy in real-time, causing delays and other challenges.

Moniruzzaman and colleagues [139] came up with a new method that merges blockchain technology with cooperative game theory to enhance user profits and guarantee secure energy transfers. This method lets customers buy, sell, and keep green energy credits on the blockchain as digital assets. A consensus mechanism among participants in blockchain energy trading helps reduce distribution line losses by using a modified Proof of Energy Generation (PoEG) protocol. The framework also has a method for forming coalitions that uses the PoEG protocol and optimisation techniques to find block miners. However, there are challenges like the potential conflict between making profits and being energy efficient, as well as higher computational demands, which could make the system less effective in encouraging the use of renewable energy.

Yapa et al. [140] came up with a Blockchain-as-a-Service for Energy Trading (BaaSET) platform that is meant for power grid applications. The platform uses reputation-based services that are carried out automatically through smart contracts on the blockchain. Reputation scores come from grid measurements, which include things like power quality and reliability indices. The platform is trying to make things more affordable and scalable to get more people involved, but as nodes come together, the lower latency might affect how accurate AI and ML decisions are. Also, the latency caused by how long it takes to generate blocks really impacts how well the consensus algorithm works, creating some challenges for the platform's reliability. Table 2.4 outlines the main characteristics of the current methods along with their drawbacks.

Table 2.4. Existing studies with their key findings

Authors	**Proposed Solution**	**Key Findings**	**Limitations**
Ghiasi et al. [134]	Hilbert-Huang Transform + Blockchain-based Ledger	Detects false data injection attacks in smart DC microgrids; retrieves	Cosine similarity-based community detection may misclassify

		voltage/current signal info; enhances security.	signals, leading to instability.
Mahmud et al. [137]	Consensus-based Distributed Control + Blockchain	Ensures cyber-resilient control of distributed energy resources (DERs); maintains power sharing and grid stability.	Blockchain-induced delays and computational costs may reduce control system responsiveness.
Liu et al. [138]	Blockchain + Wireless Networks + Dual-Chain Architecture	Promotes secure and efficient energy trading; supports renewable energy and electric vehicle integration.	High network complexity and transaction volume may cause delays in energy flow management.
Moniruzzaman et al. [139]	Blockchain + Cooperative Game Theory + Proof of Energy Generation (PoEG)	Optimizes energy trading using green credits; reduces distribution line losses; maximizes profits.	Risk of conflict between profit motives and energy efficiency; increased processing overhead.
Yapa et al. [140]	Blockchain-as-a-Service (BaaSET) + Smart Contracts + Reputation-Based Services	Decentralized platform with autonomous energy transactions based on stakeholder reputation; scalable and automated.	Latency affects AI/ML-based decisions; performance depends on block generation timing.

The traditional method has some issues because cosine similarity can be tough for the community identification server in a power grids. This could lead to vulnerabilities to cyberattacks and incorrect detections. The growing complexity of computers and their resource use might cause blockchain technology, decentralised authorisation, and encryption to slow down real-time activities and impact system performance. Having more miners could lead to shorter mining times, but the consensus processes might affect the difficulty levels. Blockchains that rely on consensus for control might experience delays and higher computational costs, which could weaken the system's resilience against cyberattacks. A blockchain-enabled energy trading system could make the network more complex and raise the number of transactions, potentially causing delays and challenges in managing energy in real-time. Latency can affect the cost and scalability of AI and ML options.

2.6. Summary of Literature Survey

The conventional techniques employed in power grids systems face several challenges that stem from the use of cosine similarity in the community identification process. This can result in vulnerabilities to cyberattacks, as the identification server may misclassify community groupings, potentially jeopardizing system stability. As the complexity of the system increases, the use of blockchain technology introduces additional concerns, such as decentralized authorization and encryption, which, while enhancing security, could slow down real-time processes. The growing demand for computational resources may lead to delays in processing, ultimately affecting the overall performance of the system. Moreover, the introduction of more miners in blockchain networks could reduce mining times, but it also leads to increased computational difficulty. This trade-off can negatively impact the efficiency of consensus-based control, which, in turn, might compromise the system's ability to withstand cyberattacks. In energy trading systems utilizing blockchain technology, the increasing complexity of the network and the growing volume of transactions can cause delays in real-time energy management. This could hinder the system's responsiveness and create challenges in ensuring the efficient allocation of resources. Additionally, latency in such systems could significantly influence the cost and scalability of AI and ML decision-making processes. As the system grows in size and complexity, these delays may become more pronounced, making it harder to maintain real-time operations and scale the system efficiently. In summary, while blockchain technologies offer improved security and decentralized control, they come with trade-offs, including increased computational overhead, latency, and the potential for inefficiencies in energy management and system scalability. These challenges must be carefully addressed to optimize the balance between security, efficiency, and performance in power grid applications.

2.7. Conclusion of Literature Survey

In conclusion, the literature on blockchain-enabled solutions for power grids, and distributed energy resources (DERs) demonstrates the significant potential of blockchain technology to enhance security, decentralization, and resilience in these systems. Blockchain facilitates secure data sharing, real-time decision-making, and the integration of renewable energy sources, while also addressing challenges such as false data injection attacks, cyber vulnerabilities, and energy management inefficiencies. However, the integration of blockchain brings along certain trade-offs, particularly in terms of computational complexity, increased latency, and system delays. As highlighted in the reviewed studies, while blockchain can improve the stability and reliability of power grids through decentralized control and consensus-based mechanisms, it can also lead to slower system responses and higher resource consumption. Furthermore, the complexity of blockchain-enabled energy trading systems may introduce difficulties in real-time management and scalability. The impact of latency on AI and machine learning models, as well as the balancing of mining difficulty levels and consensus protocols, also poses challenges to the overall efficiency of these systems. Despite these limitations, blockchain's ability to provide secure, transparent, and tamper-proof solutions positions it as a promising technology for future power grid and DER applications. Future research should focus on optimizing consensus mechanisms, reducing computational overhead, and improving real-time system performance to fully realize the benefits of blockchain while mitigating its drawbacks. Addressing these issues will be critical for advancing blockchain-based solutions and ensuring their scalability and effectiveness in energy management and cyber-resilience in power grids.

CHAPTER 3
EXTENTED PROOF-OF-VOTE (E-POV) CONSENSUS MECHANISM FOR CYBER-RESILIENT POWER GRID FRAMEWORKS

3.1. Introduction

Blockchain is an immutable distributed ledger that allows information to be stored securely without the need for a third party. Technology has garnered significant interest from researchers, particularly for its potential applications in enhancing cybersecurity within power grids. Despite various efforts to implement blockchain for data security in power grids, there remains a gap in comprehensive studies that examine blockchain's role in this area from both an application and technical perspective. Security performance is crucially impacted by factors such as fifty one percent attack tolerance, the difficulty of manipulation, and the concept of finality. For example, fifty one percent attack tolerance is typically associated with near-impossible manipulation and lack of finality, while a 33.33% attack tolerance might involve adjustable parameters and enabled finality. To address these challenges, our focus is on developing a novel approach that will deliver superior results.

3.1.1. Consensus Mechanism in Blockchain

Consensus is a fundamental concept in distributed systems overall and is not limited to just blockchain technology. This can be applied in cases where multiple processes or nodes need to keep the same state of a data item at the same time. There are two main types of blockchains: permission-less and permissioned. Anonymous nodes are those in a blockchain that can be accessed without permission. A fork might occur from the insertion of a tampered-with new transaction block. When an invalid transaction conflicts with an authorized one, a fork occurs. To achieve consensus across network nodes in which they all agree on a single value as being the right one is the fundamental goal of a consensus method. Nodes in a permissioned blockchain are not anonymous; rather, they are regarded as recognized entities.

However, since the nodes cannot be trusted, a consensus remains to be reached in order fix the issue. Fig.3.1 depicts the Consensus distributed environment architecture in blockchain. It's really important to think about reaching a consensus, especially when some nodes in a network aren't working right or are having trouble communicating consistently. We can agree on different types of failures that could occur in distributed systems. Additionally, the type of communication model—whether synchronous or asynchronous—that is used in creating a consensus system is considered. There are various kinds of failures, such as temporal failure, byzantine failure, security failure, omission failure, crash failure, transient failure, and environmental perturbations. The explanation of these failures are explained below.

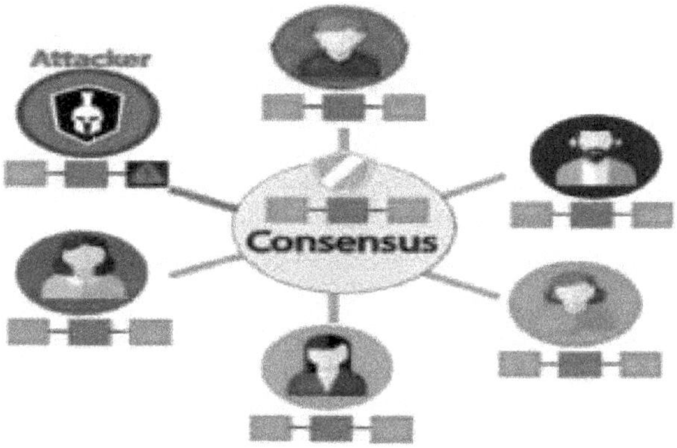

Fig.3.1. Consensus in distributed environment

- A crash failure happens when a process stops working completely and can't come back, resulting in a permanent stop. In a synchronous environment, you can detect this kind of failure by using timeout mechanisms because the system can keep track of when a process doesn't respond within a set timeframe. Detecting crash failures in an asynchronous environment is really tough because there's no global time coordination. This makes it hard to tell if a process is just slow or if it has actually failed. This uncertainty makes it harder to design fault-tolerant systems in asynchronous environments, which means we need to use more advanced techniques to make sure they are reliable.
- Transient failure: These issues are unpredictable and can be lasting, which means they might happen at random times and continue until they are fixed. In

hardware, faults can happen due to problems like weak batteries or power surges, which can interrupt normal operations and might lead to lasting damage. On the software side, these issues could come from rare bugs in the internal code, which can be especially troublesome since they might not be caught during testing. Software bugs can cause unexpected behaviour or system failures, which makes them tough to find and fix. So, both hardware and software issues can really affect how reliable and stable a system is.

- Omission failure happens when there are problems with gearbox, like buffer overflow. This occurs when the system can't keep up with the incoming data at the needed speed. Collisions are another frequent issue that occurs when several data packets are sent at the same time, which can result in data loss or corruption. Also, if the transmitter isn't working properly, it can mess up the communication process, leading to incomplete or wrong data being sent, which can really affect how reliable the network is.
- Security issues happen when there are targeted attacks and impersonation, which can create major weaknesses in a system. These breaches can lead to unauthorised access to sensitive information, which can let bad actors manipulate or corrupt data. Data corruption can really mess things up, affecting how systems work and possibly causing important information to be lost or services to be disrupted.
- Byzantine failure is when different parts of a system get conflicting information, causing each part to observe different symptoms. This difference makes it hard for the system to come to an agreement, since the conflicting information causes confusion among the members [141]. For example, one person might think a server is down, while someone else sees it as working just fine. The conflicting data means that we can't definitely say the server has failed, which makes it hard for everyone to agree on what happened.
- Temporal failure happens when a system doesn't meet a certain deadline, leading to delays that make the result not useful. Sometimes, the system can give the right answers, but if they come too late, they aren't helpful or important anymore. This kind of failure is really important in real-time systems because timing is crucial for how applications work properly. In these situations, even small delays can cause big problems, affecting the system's overall reliability

and performance. Therefore, tackling temporal failures is really important when designing and optimising real-time systems [141].

- Environmental perturbations happen when a solution isn't properly adjusted to the changes in the environment. If the solution isn't flexible, it might not adapt to new situations, making results that were once correct no longer accurate. As things change, sticking to a fixed solution can become outdated, resulting in mistakes that could have been prevented with a more flexible and adaptable method. This shows how crucial it is to make sure that solutions are created to adapt and stay accurate despite continuous changes in the environment [142].

Blockchains operate as a self-sufficient, decentralised record-keeping system that is not controlled by any one organisation. Some people might really want to find ways to create vulnerabilities. So, it's really important for blockchain to consider the Byzantine problem and how to solve it. A Byzantine fault occurs when different parts of the system experience the issue in various ways. It makes it harder to agree on anything. This means that the system struggles to bounce back from mistakes and is more likely to encounter them. For instance, a server that one individual thinks is not working properly might actually be functioning just fine for someone else. The server can't get a negative rating because the observers don't all agree. The term "Byzantine" originates from the "general's difficulty" associated with the Byzantine Empire. It's a deadlock in negotiations with several generals surrounding a city. The generals need to come up with a strategy for attacking the city. The choice to either pull back or move forward will depend on the individual commander. It's really important for all generals to come to the same decision. Issues arise when one general betrays the others in the group. Choosing to vote for a plan that isn't great, which leads to division, is really a betrayal. Consider the scenario of eleven generals, where ten are completely reliable and one is a traitor. If there's a tie, the traitor will talk to both sides, giving an attack vote to the supporters and a retreat vote to the others. In this situation, one half of the army would pull back, while the other half would move forward. Solving a consensus problem in asynchronous networks is really challenging. A lot of randomised consensus methods have been suggested in the literature to tackle this issue. The methods make three key characteristics of Byzantine consensus—agreement, termination, and validity—optional instead of essential. Some popular examples of randomised techniques are the Rabin consensus algorithm and the Ben-Or consensus algorithm. There are various types of randomness-based consensus algorithms, including Las Vegas and Monte Carlo. In another type of consensus process, the probability is decided by a chosen leader. The feature of relaxed validity allows for additional categorisation of Monte Carlo consensus. Using a randomised technique to achieve consensus can compromise the security of distributed systems. The most common types of consensus algorithms are leader-based, leader-free, deterministic, Monte Carlo, Las Vegas, and randomised. Each approach is categorised into synchronous, partial synchronous, and asynchronous models of communication. Randomised consensus can help ensure validity, termination, and agreement, but there are some limitations to its effectiveness. Some solutions are deterministic, meaning they don't involve any probabilities. The Monte Carlo approach is run independently on each process or node using a set of range data to achieve consensus. The global consensus value is determined by averaging values obtained from multiple procedures. In Las Vegas, each round of consensus comes with a specific probability. The clocks in Las Vegas and Monte Carlo show different times. Unlike Las Vegas, where everything feels like a gamble, the timing in Monte Carlo is much more predictable. Consensus procedures that are based on a leader can enable the ending of consensus. Additionally, we present a method for achieving consensus without a designated leader. Fig.3.1 shows the basic structure of distributed systems, and Fig.3.2 gives a detailed look at consensus methods.

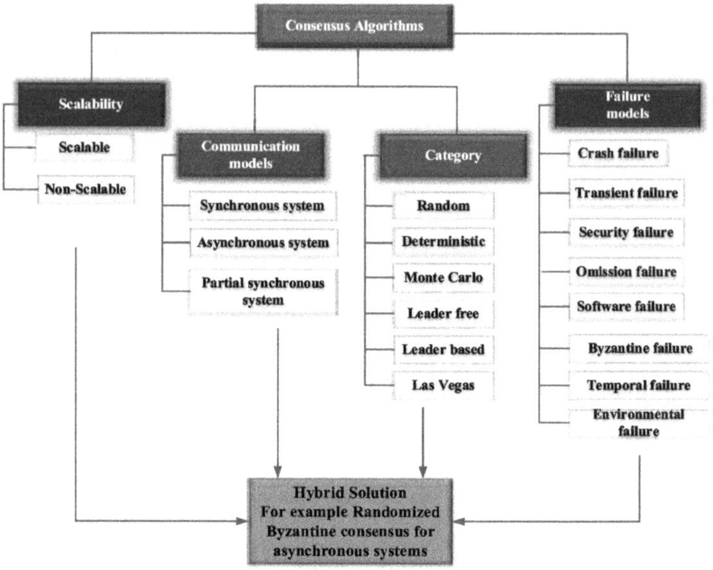

Fig.3.2. Detailing of consensus methods

In addition to the overall classification of consensus algorithms used in distributed systems, we can specifically divide the consensus mechanisms in blockchain into two primary categories: proof-based consensus and vote-based consensus. In proof-based consensus, a node that wants to join the network has to show its qualifications, proving that it can do a better job than others at adding new blocks. In vote-based consensus, every node in the network needs to talk to each other and share its verification results for a new transaction block with all the other nodes. The final choice to add a block happens only when most of the nodes come to a consensus on the outcome.

Comparisons of consensus algorithms is given in table 3.1 based on the study on various parameters like type of blockchain, scalability of the framework, performance of system, consensus finality etc.

Table 3.1. Comparison Analysis of Consensus Algorithms

Parameter	Description
Blockchain Type	Classified into public, private, and consortium. Impacts membership control and should align with business application needs.
Scalability	This shows how well the system can manage more nodes and transactions. ELASTICO and PoT can scale well, while PoW and Implicit Consensus cannot.
Adversary Tolerance Model	Identifies a part of the network that can withstand faults or attacks. ELASTICO offers excellent control over adversaries.
Performance-Related Parameters	A lot of algorithms don't have experimental evaluation. We have tested ELASTICO for latency, throughput, and bandwidth.
Communication Model and Complexity	Synchronous vs. asynchronous models. ELASTICO and Leader-Free use synchronous; PoW, PoT, Ripple use asynchronous. Leader-Free has linear communication cost.
Attacks	Ripple is vulnerable to Sybil attacks. PoT and Leader-Free are secure. Most others need further analysis.
Energy Consumption	Energy usage not experimentally evaluated for most algorithms, creating a gap in understanding efficiency.
Mining and Consensus Category	Defines mining process: proof-based for large networks (e.g., PoW, ELASTICO), vote-based for smaller networks.
Consensus Finality	Finality types: probabilistic and absolute. ELASTICO, PoPF, and Implicit Consensus offer absolute finality.

3.2. Motivation

According to earlier studies, the PoV consensus blockchain seems like a promising option for improving the data security of existing power systems. Our previous research found a vulnerability related to fifty one percent attacks in both blockchain and power grid systems. After looking into how well the system works against possible attacks, we discovered that it is quite strong. We think that using meters as nodes in a distributed network, with meter data encoded as blocks, could really improve the resilience and security of the power grid. Adding PoV to the suggested distributed blockchain for power grid networks enhances security and makes it more resistant to cyber-attacks. Future research will aim to improve security against cyber threats while also ensuring privacy protection and meeting regulatory requirements, which will ultimately boost the performance of the blockchain system using PoV consensus. As a result, we are focusing on an Extended PoV approach to enhance the privacy and confidentiality needs of personal information.

3.3. Objective

This work proposes an Extended Proof-Of-Vote (PoV) Consensus mechanism designed to enhance the resilience and consistency of blockchain frameworks. Our approach integrates the strengths of both PoW and Proof-Of-Vote, the text has been corrected to state that PoW provides **integrity and Sybil-resistance**, not confidentiality. The implementation of PoW as a "Gatekeeper" for the voting process has. By adopting this hybrid approach, the generated blockchains and the votes collected and tallied within the system are secure and protected. Our method outlines specific conditions necessary to safely and effectively update the consensus process in a PoW-based blockchain. This proposal aims to enhance the security of the consensus mechanism by reducing the risk of existing attack vectors and preventing the emergence of new ones. PoW, rooted in the robust cryptographic foundations of blockchain systems, ensures security and confidentiality through the trusted environment of commissioner nodes. Incorporating the PoV into this system adds an additional layer of security by utilizing a voting process within consortium blockchains. While traditional consensus methods may compromise performance for the sake of security, our approach offers improved blockchain efficiency with reduced transaction identification delays under secure conditions. The use of Proof-Of-Vote ensures that each node's input is considered, creating a more democratic and secure framework for the blockchain system. Fig.3.3 illustrates the sequential process of the Extended Proof-Of-Vote (EPoV) consensus mechanism within the blockchain network. The dotted blue box represents the blockchain network, where each node symbolizes an individual participant in the network. Commissioner nodes, identified as special nodes, play a crucial role in verifying transactions and ensuring security through the Proof-of-Work (PoW) mechanism. The dotted red box outlines the EPoV consensus process. In this phase, nodes within the network cast their votes on transaction blocks, and these votes are collected and counted to establish consensus. Subsequently, the commissioner nodes perform PoW to validate the transactions and blocks. Upon successful verification, new blocks are created and appended to the blockchain. The security layer depicts the cryptographic mechanisms employed to maintain confidentiality and security within the network. Finally, the green dotted box signifies the consensus mechanisms. In this stage, all unverified transactions are compiled into a transaction pool, where votes are cast, and PoW is executed by the commissioner nodes. After obtaining majority approval and verifying with PoW, the block is finalized and added to the blockchain. Additionally, the attack prevention mechanisms illustrate how the system mitigates existing attack vectors and prevents the emergence of new ones. This diagram effectively provides a clear visual representation of the Extended PoV Consensus mechanism, emphasizing the integration of PoW and PoV processes, the security measures in place, and the overall flow of the consensus and block creation process.

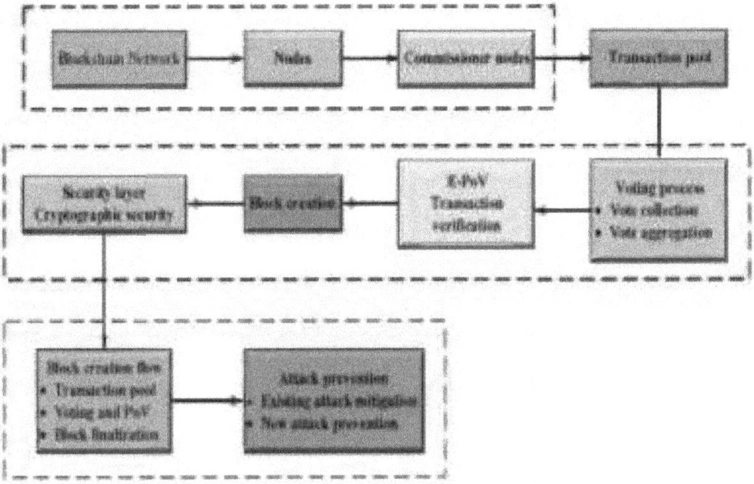

Fig.3.3. Flowchart for E-PoV consensus mechanism

3.4. Research Methodology

This section describes our work in depth, including the strategies we employed, the problem definition, the consensus mechanism, and the techniques we used. The models that are used in this technique are as follows.

3.4.1. Techniques used

Problem Definition: The PoV consensus mechanism proposed by the consortium blockchain is estimated to fulfil the following requirements.

Consistency: The consistency requirement mandates that all nodes within the consortium blockchain maintain identical copies of the blockchain data, allowing them to converge on a consistent final state while providing a unified external service. In the PoV consensus mechanism, the integrity and tamper-resistance of transactions are assured through the validation of a single block that achieves consensus termination. This approach simplifies the consensus process, as nodes can reach an agreement on the validity of transactions without needing to verify multiple blocks, thereby enhancing reliability and reducing the potential for inconsistencies in the blockchain data.

Availability: Availability is a crucial requirement, ensuring that the system's services remain accessible at all times, which is facilitated by the efficiency of the consensus mechanism. The PoV consensus model guarantees that the system can respond to every operational request within a defined timeframe. By optimizing the parameter values, PoV ensures that the consensus process can function effectively and generate new blocks within a finite time period, thereby minimizing delays and ensuring continuous service availability.

Partition Tolerance: It states the ability of the distributed system to continue providing services even when it experiences network partitions or breakdowns. The PoV mechanism is designed to handle partitions to a certain extent, based on specific security assumptions. In scenarios where network partitions occur, PoV can maintain operational integrity by allowing nodes to continue validating transactions and achieving consensus among the remaining connected nodes. This capability is indispensable for guaranteeing the blockchain network's overall functionality and dependability, regardless of unexpected interruptions.

Efficiency: Efficiency is very important for the PoV consensus mechanism, highlighting the need for really high throughput. Throughput refers to the total number of transactions that are executed in a given time period, and it plays a vital role in the performance of the blockchain network. The PoV mechanism aims to increase throughput by simplifying the consensus process and reducing the resources needed for validating transactions. By concentrating on improving the consensus parameters and making sure block generation is quick, PoV boosts the system's overall performance, allowing it to manage a higher volume of transactions effectively.

3.4.2. Proof of Vote

It gives a detailed explanation of PoV consensus algorithm, highlighting its superior effectiveness over existing methods in areas such as security, resource consumption, transaction throughput, and transaction confirmation time. The PoV consensus design categorizes nodes into four distinct roles: commissioner, butler, butler candidate, and ordinary user, each playing a specific part in the consensus process. The different roles collaborate to improve the overall efficiency and security of the blockchain network. Fig.3.4 visually represents the various functions and interactions within the PoV system, illustrating how these roles contribute to the consensus procedure.

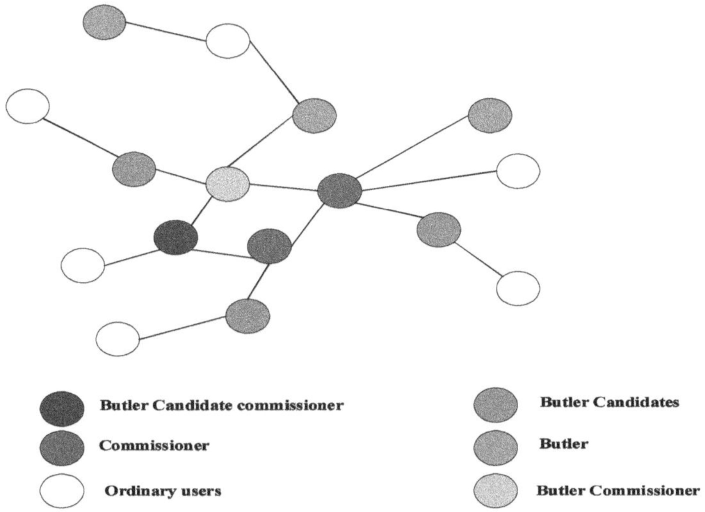

Fig.3.4 Roles in PoV

Commissioner: A consortium committee made up of several firms or organisations from around the world works together to run a consortium blockchain system. A commissioner is a major member of this body, and he or she may also serve in other roles within the system. To join the network, a new commissioner must be authorised under the consortium's regulations and recognised by a blockchain node. Commissioners supervise butlers by making recommendations, voting, and evaluating their performance. They are also in charge of sending and validating data blocks. Newly produced blocks are broadcast to all commissioners on the blockchain network for verification. A block is declared genuine and uploaded to the blockchain when it receives a majority of votes, indicating the agreement of all commissioners.

Butlers: These are specialised nodes that are in charge of producing blocks on the blockchain. The number of Butler nodes is limited. The PoV method separates the duties of voting and bookkeeping. Butlers are in charge of block generation, whilst commissioners handle voting. Butlers, like Bitcoin miners, are chosen at random by the consensus rules to produce a block without having to waste processing resources. A butler's responsibilities include collecting network transactions, arranging them into blocks, and signing the blocks. Commissioners vote on candidates for the butler team. Butlers take turns producing blocks in a random order throughout their term and may run for re-election when it ends. A node can function as both a commissioner and a butler. To become a butler, you must first register as a candidate and then win the election.

Butler Candidate: Due to the limited number of butlers, commissioners choose butlers from a pool of candidates by election. Butler candidates who are not elected may remain online and wait until the next election. To become a butler candidate, you must first create a user ID on the consortium platform and apply for the position, then submit a dated and signed recommendation letter from at least one commissioner (the letter is generated using an asymmetric encryption function and encrypted with the private key to prevent forgery), and finally make the required deposit. Commissioners can also hold two positions: commissioner and butler candidate.

Ordinary Users: Ordinary users can access and exit the system at any time without requiring permission. While using the system's services, they can observe the complete consensus process. Ordinary users participate in the block forwarding process and can submit transactions during the block generating phase. Fig.3.5 depicts the relationships and interactions between various roles in the PoV system, including commissioners, butlers, butler candidates, and ordinary users. This picture clarifies how each position contributes to the consensus process and the general operation of the blockchain network by emphasising the interconnectedness of their tasks and the flow of information inside the system.

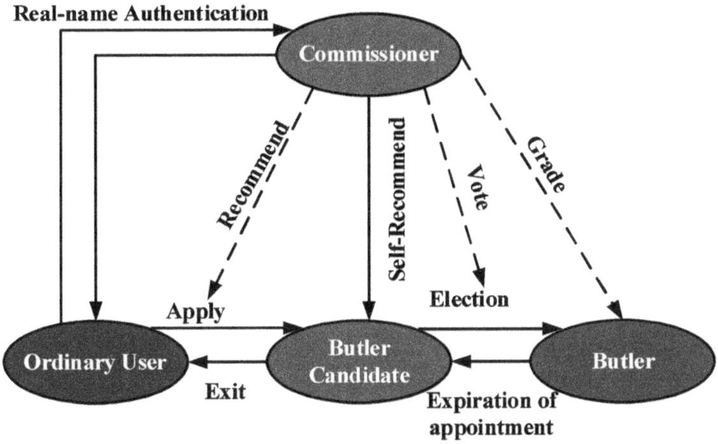

Fig.3.5. Conversion of four roles

The PoV consensus mechanism introduces a flexible node access and representation system that effectively reduces communication complexity, which in turn greatly enhances how well the blockchain network can grow and handle more users. When nodes are given the chance to connect to the network and take part in consensus processes in a streamlined manner, PoV ensures that the network can handle an increasing number of participants without a corresponding increase in communication overhead. This flexibility is crucial for maintaining efficiency as the network grows. Moreover, PoV's design balances the roles of nodes, allowing for efficient management of resources while maintaining high levels of security and consensus accuracy. Despite the inherent limitation posed by the serial production of blocks, PoV mitigates this challenge by optimizing block creation and validation processes. As a result, the network can sustain higher throughput while ensuring that the blockchain remains secure and tamper-resistant. This combination of scalability, efficiency, and security makes PoV a robust solution for modern blockchain networks.

3.4.3. Experimental Setup

This section outlines the experimental methodology applied to evaluate the proposed E-PoV approach, which incorporates both consensus and voting mechanisms.

Consensus Process

Let N_c denote the number of commissioners, N_b the number of active butlers, N_{bc} the butler candidates, and N_o the ordinary users. The total count of participating roles is expressed as N_{all}. Since a node can serve in multiple roles simultaneously, the condition $N_{all} \leq N_c + N_b + N_{bc} + N_o$ holds true, with N_b being a fixed value.

Each butler is assigned an identifier from 0 to N_b for every term. Typically, the candidate pool N_{bc} is larger than the available butler slots. In cases where $N_{bc} < N_b$, the allocation process redistributes certain identifiers to maintain system continuity. For instance, if $N_b = 8$ and $N_{bc} = 6$, the identifiers are assigned as: {B1, B2, B3, B4, B5, B6, B1, B2} for positions 0 to 7. In such a scenario, butlers B_1 and B_2, having secured the highest votes, each hold two identifiers.

A butler's operational term lasts T_w, during which $B_w + 1$ valid blocks are generated. The final block of the term contains details of the butler elections and associated records. For any block to be recognized as valid, it must receive at least $\left\lceil \frac{N_c}{2} \right\rceil + 1$ signatures from distinct commissioners. Within each packing interval T_b, the designated butler must produce a valid block within the given time frame. The consensus flow throughout a single term is illustrated in Fig.3.6.

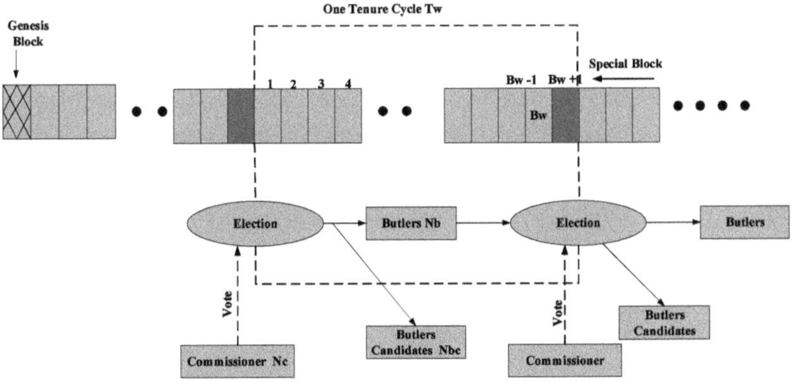

Fig.3.6. One round

Consensus Process in a Tenure

In each consensus round, the designated butler is responsible for producing a valid block. A complete tenure consists of $B_w + 1$ consensus rounds, thereby generating $B_w + 1$ valid blocks. At the end of each round, the current butler executes a procedure to generate a random integer R. The duty of producing the next block in the upcoming consensus round is assigned to the butler whose identifier matches R.

If the assigned butler fails to produce a valid block within the allocated time T_b, the task is transferred to the $(R + 1)^{th}$ butler. In this case, the value of R is updated according to:

$$R = R + 1 \; mod \; N_b$$

Consensus is successfully achieved as long as at least one butler functions correctly during the process. Since only one block can obtain the required majority of signatures within any single packing cycle T_b, the blockchain remains consistent and avoids the occurrence of forks.

The final block in each tenure, denoted as the $(B_w + 1)^{th}$ block, serves a special purpose. During this final consensus round, the current butlers and butler candidates compete for positions in the upcoming tenure. The N_b candidates receiving the highest number of votes are elected as the new butlers. Each commissioner submits a voting list, and the election results, along with relevant supporting data, are permanently recorded in this special block. Once the block is finalized, the serving butlers retire, and the newly elected butlers assume their roles for the next tenure.

Voting Process

The "Proof of Vote" (PoV) mechanism forms the foundation of the consensus process and incorporates two distinct voting procedures, as illustrated in Fig.3.7. The first pertains to validating newly produced blocks, while the second is used for selecting the team of butlers for the upcoming tenure. In both cases, commissioners participate by providing digitally signed approvals.

Proof of Vote on Blocks

When a butler B_i generates a block, it is broadcast to all commissioners for validation. A commissioner who approves the block encrypts its header and timestamp, signs them, and sends the signed data back to B_i collects at least $\left\lceil \frac{N_c}{2} \right\rceil + 1$ signatures within the predefined time limit, the block is considered valid. Otherwise, the block is deemed invalid, and the next butler B_{i+1} assumes responsibility for regenerating it.

Digital Signature (for authenticity) and **Selective Payload Encryption** (for privacy). The Block Header remains partially transparent to allow public verification of the signature, while sensitive meter data is encrypted. Computation overhead is now quantified in Table 3.2, showing a negligible 5% increase in validation time.

Proof of Vote on Butlers

In the final consensus round of a tenure, commissioners submit signed voting transactions to the acting butler B_i. After aggregating and counting the votes, B_i generates a special block containing the election outcomes and all related records, which is then sent to commissioners for verification.

Commissioners' votes are expressed through two types of tickets:

1. **Score Tickets:** Each commissioner maintains a score list for all butler candidates and selects the sequence of candidates starting from the highest-scoring ones.
2. **Designated Tickets:** Commissioners may select specific candidates based on subjective judgment or random choice, thereby enhancing the diversity and adaptability of the butler set.

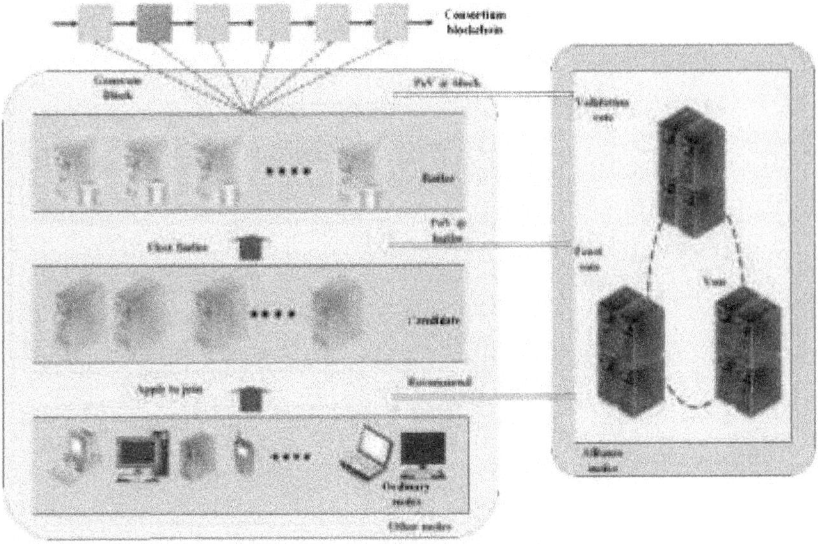

Fig.3.7. Two kinds of proof of vote

Excitation mechanism

Butler candidates have the option to withdraw their candidacy at any time, upon which they can reclaim their deposit. However, if a butler chooses to leave the network during its active tenure, the deposit cannot be refunded. In every transaction, both participating parties are required to pay transaction fees. These fees act as an incentive for the butler who successfully includes the transaction in a block. Each commissioner maintains a list of active butler candidates and evaluates their performance according to predefined scoring criteria:

- When a commissioner approves and signs a block, the designated duty butler for that block earns additional points. If the block is rejected, the butler's score is reduced.
- If a butler is offline and misses the opportunity to produce a block, its score is reset to zero, requiring the butler to rebuild its score upon returning online.

Scoring may differ among commissioners for the same butler, as levels of trust vary. These scores play a critical role during the voting process. At the conclusion of a tenure, both butlers and butler candidates are rewarded by the consortium in proportion to the number of valid blocks they have produced. This reward structure motivates them to carry out their responsibilities diligently, act with integrity, and remain consistently online.

3.4.4. Object of study

The current platforms have a number of limitations, including modular design, parallel computing, and privacy protection. In our analytical article, we use extended proof of vote to get beyond the privacy protection. By integrating PoW's **computational immutability** and **Sybil-resistance** with PoV's stakeholder-based finality, the framework achieves. The generated blockchains and the votes that are gathered and counted are secure and safe when using our proposed methods. We outline some conditions in order to update a PoW blockchain's consensus mechanism in a safe, profitable, and smooth manner. By reducing known attack vectors and blocking new ones, the plan should increase the security of our consensus. In essence, the system must be incentive-compatible, meaning that voters and commissioners should gain by adhering to the consensus rules while losing out if they do not. Depending on the cryptographic underpinning of blockchain systems, PoW ensures its safety & confidentiality by utilising the secure and reliable surroundings of the commissioner nodes. In this work, a full consensus model based on voting processes & consortium blockchains is provided. The existing consensus technique sacrifices performance to ensure security because security and availability are so important. Under safety-assured settings, our approach may offer high block chain efficiency & minimal transaction identification delays. We will examine the validity of POV in this section, which can be influenced by two factors: the incentive system and the voting process. According to this, ordinary nodes are attempting to join the candidate block before choosing to join the butler side. We create blocks on the butler side using our consortium algorithm. Votes generated by the commissioner are sent to the consortium blocks after the blocks have been generated, and the proposed EPoV method is then used to secure the votes in the consortium blocks. Our major goal is to secure or protect the votes and blocks that the commissioners and voters have produced and are registered in the proof of vote.

3.4.5. Performance Proof and Analysis

This study introduces an advanced consensus algorithm tailored for consortium blockchains, built upon a structured voting mechanism. Unlike many existing algorithms that sacrifice performance for heightened security, the PoV approach leverages the trusted nature of consortium nodes alongside an optimized decision-making process. This combination reduces transaction validation delays while maintaining accuracy, thereby boosting overall blockchain performance.

Consistency: PoV achieves consensus finality with just one block confirmation, ensuring that transactions cannot be maliciously altered once validated.

Availability: PoV ensures the steady generation of valid blocks by butlers, provided appropriate system parameters are maintained. This guarantees prompt responses to user requests.

Partition Tolerance: PoV can sustain functionality during network partitions, provided more than half of the commissioners and at least one honest butler remains connected.

Security

Lemma 3.1: Let there be Nc commissioners. Blocks remain valid and secure if more than $\left\lceil \frac{N_c}{2} \right\rceil + 1$ commissioners are operational.

Proof: If illicit blocks could be validated, it would mean they obtained more than $\left\lceil \frac{N_c}{2} \right\rceil + 1$ commissioner signatures. However, honest commissioners will not sign an invalid block, meaning the maximum possible signatures on such a block is $N_c - (\left\lceil \frac{N_c}{2} \right\rceil + 1) = \left\lceil \frac{N_c}{2} \right\rceil - 1$, making successful validation impossible.

Consistency

Lemma 3.2: If a block $Block_h$ at height h is valid, it confirms that all preceding transactions from $\{Block_o, Block_1, \ldots\ldots Block_{h-1}\}$ are final and immutable.

Proof: Using mathematical induction:

Base Case (h=0): $Block_0$ is the genesis block, signed by all commissioners, ensuring consistency.

Induction Step (h=1): A valid $Block_1$ means over half the commissioners verified and signed $Block_0$'s pre-block, confirming consistency.

Induction Step (h=k+1): A valid $Block_{k+1}$ contains signatures from over half the commissioners, confirming the validity and consistency of $Block_k$ and all preceding blocks.

The integrated scoring and voting system prevents malicious butlers from influencing consensus. Low-performing butlers naturally lose their positions due to reduced scores and minimal rewards, making sustained participation unprofitable.

3.5. Results and Discussion

The success of the proposed approach is thoroughly examined, where various metrics and performance indicators are evaluated to assess its effectiveness. The implementation of the proposed technique is executed using the Python framework, which provides a versatile and powerful environment for developing machine learning and signal processing applications. The system configuration for the suggested solution is designed to optimize performance and ensure smooth operation. It is built on a 64-bit operating system, enabling efficient handling of large datasets and execution of complex computations often required in signal processing tasks. To support the demanding requirements of the proposed method, the system is equipped with 16.0 GB of RAM. Overall, this configuration is specifically tailored to meet the technical demands of the proposed approach, ensuring that the system operates effectively in various scenarios.

3.5.1. Potential applications of the results

Intriguing prospects for applications in physics and other natural sciences are presented by the Extended Proof of Vote (EPoV) architecture that proposed in this analytical study. Here are some possible uses for such a system:

Scientific Research Collaboration: In scientific research collaborations, EPoV could be used to safeguard and authenticate votes and blocks in consortium blockchains. Transparency and integrity in scientific research might be ensured by employing EPoV to securely preserve and verify study findings, experimental data, and even peer review procedures.

Data Integrity in Environmental Monitoring: EPoV could be used in environmental research domains to protect sensor-derived data that tracks several environmental characteristics like biodiversity, water quality, and air quality. EPoV has the potential to bolster confidence in environmental monitoring initiatives and facilitate evidence-based decision-making for environmental conservation and management by guaranteeing the validity and integrity of data held on consortium blockchains.

Secure Data Sharing in Astronomy: Researchers and observatories may benefit from the safe exchange and validation of astronomical data through the use of EPoV. Collaboration and data integrity within the astronomy community might be ensured by storing observational data, computational models, and catalogs of celestial objects in consortium blockchains using EPoV.

Blockchain-based Particle Physics Experiments: EPoV has the potential to safeguard and validate data produced by particle physics experiments carried out at massive colliders. Using consortium blockchains with EPoV, scientists could safely store and exchange experimental data, promoting cooperation and guaranteeing the accuracy of results in particle physics research.

Securing Genetic Data in Biology: Biology-related consortium blockchains storing genetic data may be protected and verified with EPoV. With the use of EPoV, genetic sequences, gene expression profiles, and genomic variants might be safely captured, improving data privacy and integrity for uses in personalized medicine and genetic research.

The proposed EPoV architecture presents a viable method for safeguarding votes and blocks in consortium blockchains, with possible applications across a range of physics and other natural scientific areas. By guaranteeing data confidentiality, transparency, and integrity, EPoV may help to advance scientific cooperation and study in these areas.

3.6. Conclusion

The PoV consensus algorithm offers several advantages over traditional PoW and BFT-based algorithms. Unlike PoW, PoV requires only one block confirmation to secure tamper-proof transactions, enabling improved performance without compromising security. Additionally, PoV's communication complexity is significantly lower than that of BFT-based algorithms, making it more efficient and scalable as the number of committee nodes increases. PoV also reduces energy consumption, as it does not rely on extensive computation or specialized hardware.

Moreover, PoV supports the regular rotation of consensus nodes, mitigating the risk of single points of failure and preventing long-term control by attackers. The algorithm is flexible enough to accommodate government and regulatory oversight, allowing for modifications to the blockchain when necessary, with the consent of the majority of committee members. PoV offers a promising alternative to traditional consensus algorithms, combining enhanced performance with robust security and lower energy consumption. While the need for dynamic adjustment of waiting times presents a challenge, PoV's flexibility and efficiency make it well-suited for consortium blockchain environments where regulatory oversight and adaptability are crucial.

CHAPTER 4

DISTRIBUTED BLOCKCHAIN FRAMEWORK FOR FIFTY ONE PERCENT ATTACK PROTECTION IN POWER GRIDS

4.1. Introduction

Cybersecurity is an essential concern across both industry and academia, driving the adoption of various monitoring and defence strategies to strengthen the resilience of modern SG technologies. To address this, a Blockchain-based cybersecurity management system has been developed, leveraging the collective power of the community to identify and mitigate vulnerabilities. This approach proposes a distributed Blockchain solution designed to protect SGs from cyber threats, utilizing meter nodes and Blockchain technology to improve the reliability and safety of smart energy systems. By incorporating cryptographic methods such as the Schnorr signature, the system ensures the integrity and confidentiality of digital communications, offering a secure way to create and validate digital signatures. Additionally, the Whirlpool hash algorithm is employed to efficiently condense data within the current block, optimizing information processing. The implementation is carried out using PYTHON technology, and its effectiveness is assessed through various performance metrics, including probability mass functions, cumulative distribution functions with chi-square and non-central chi-square distributions, as well as latency and throughput analysis. Overall, the proposed solution offers key advantages, including low resource consumption, fast transaction confirmation times, enhanced security, and improved throughput, outperforming existing consensus algorithms.

4.2. Motivation

Blockchain technology, being independent of any centralized authority, offers a decentralized and immutable distributed ledger capable of securely storing data. This unique feature has gained significant attention in various sectors, particularly in the field of microgrid cybersecurity, where it is seen as a promising solution to address vulnerabilities in SG systems. Despite numerous efforts to integrate

Blockchain technology for enhancing cybersecurity in SGs, challenges remain in fully leveraging its potential, especially in the context of protecting critical infrastructure from sophisticated cyber threats. Blockchain, when used in this capacity, acts as a robust "firewall" that prevents unauthorized access and data manipulation, making it a valuable tool for securing sensitive information within smart energy systems. While The applicability of Blockchain in SGs has been the subject of numerous studies and other sectors, a significant gap exists in addressing the specific challenge of the "fifty one percent attack," a critical vulnerability in Blockchain-based systems. A fifty one percent attack is triggered when a malicious actor obtains control of the majority of nodes in the network, thereby enabling them to manipulate the consensus mechanism, and in turn, alter the validity of transactions. This threat is particularly concerning in public Blockchain networks where a large number of participants are involved. Despite its theoretical risks, launching a successful fifty one percent attack on a well-distributed public Blockchain system is difficult due to the need to manage most of the network's computing capabilities. However, its potential impact on the integrity and reliability of systems, such as power grids, cannot be underestimated.

This research seeks to address this pressing issue by proposing a decentralized, Blockchain-based information security paradigm that specifically targets the vulnerabilities associated with fifty one percent attacks. Unlike previous studies that focus on general cybersecurity measures or broader Blockchain implementations, this approach is uniquely designed to reduce the risks from these attacks while improving the security and strength of power grid systems. This study looks at new ways to make sure data is accurate, consensus is reliable, and systems are strong, aiming to address a gap in the current research and provide a more secure solution for Blockchain-based cybersecurity in critical infrastructure. The proposed system would not only protect against traditional cyber threats but also offer a fortified defense against one of the most significant and challenging attack vectors in decentralized systems.

4.3. Proposed distributed blockchain framework against cyber attacks

The proposed approach employs blockchain technology to monitor and record system transactions within the Smart Grid (SG) network using a consensus-driven mechanism. Blockchain is a decentralized and distributed ledger framework that securely stores data while ensuring transparency and immutability. It comprises a sequence of time-stamped, tamper-resistant data files that together create a digital ledger accessible to multiple participants. This ledger can be updated and verified collaboratively, eliminating the need for a central authority.

Each "block" in the ledger holds a collection of transaction records, which are arranged chronologically to form a continuous "chain." These blocks are connected through cryptographic hash functions, safeguarding the integrity and authenticity of the stored data. Information in each block typically includes transaction details such as sender and receiver identities, date and time stamps, and specifics about the exchanged value or assets. When a new block is generated, it is linked to its predecessor via its hash, ensuring the entire chain remains consistent and secure.

Once recorded, data on the blockchain cannot be modified, which guarantees a high degree of trust and security among network participants. Through this decentralized structure, blockchain technology enables reliable, transparent, and tamper-proof transaction tracking in the SG network, thereby improving the system's overall integrity and dependability.

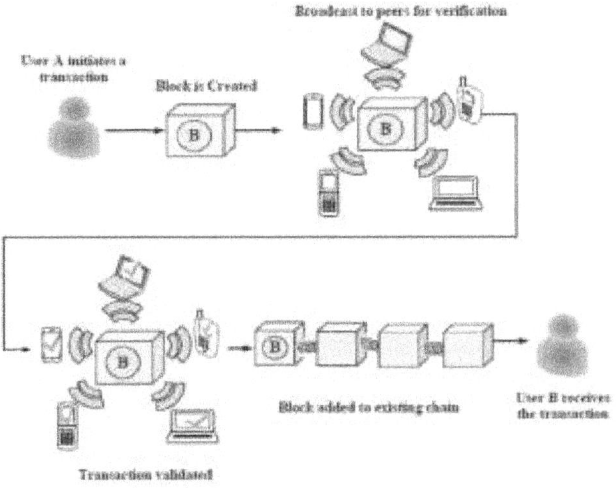

Fig.4.1. Working mechanism of Blockchain

Fig.4.1 depicts how blockchain technology functions in a typical transaction workflow [144]. In this scenario, although user B was originally intended to perform the transaction, it is initiated by user A. Once initiated, the transaction details are stored in a newly generated data block, which becomes part of the blockchain. This block is then distributed to all nodes (peers) in the network for verification. Each peer independently validates the transaction to confirm its authenticity. If a majority of nodes approve it, the new block is permanently added to the blockchain, and the updated ledger is synchronized across all peers, ensuring transparency and redundancy. Because the system is decentralized, no single authority controls the blockchain. Every meter node in the network is assigned a public–private key pair: the public key serves as its visible identifier, while the private key authenticates the node and authorizes its actions. This cryptographic pairing prevents unauthorized access and ensures that only valid transactions are recorded.

Before transmitting any data between nodes, encryption is applied to safeguard privacy and security. In the proposed framework's final stage, all validated information is securely stored in a distributed ledger format, where each data block is cryptographically linked to the previous one. This block-by-block connection makes the stored data tamper-resistant. The transmitted data includes both plaintext content and digital signatures generated using the Schnorr signature algorithm. This cryptographic method enhances security by providing a reliable and efficient way to authenticate transactions and maintain the integrity of the recorded data throughout the blockchain network. As a result, the system produces a transparent, immutable, and secure log of all activities, preserving the reliability of the power grid's data.

To further strengthen blockchain security, cryptographic hash functions link each block, generating a unique and irreversible representation of its contents. These functions compress and transform the input into a fixed-length hash value, or message digest, which can be used to verify data integrity. In the proposed system, the Whirlpool hash algorithm is adopted. Whirlpool is an iterative, one-way cryptographic function known for its robust message digest output and flexibility in handling inputs up to 2^{256} bits, producing a fixed 512-bit digest.

In the transaction sequence, user A sends the request to user B, who then receives and verifies it. Relevant transaction data is compiled into a new block, which is added to the existing blockchain, preserving the chronological and secure order of records. This block is then broadcast across the network for further verification, where consensus is achieved through a distributed, address-based voting process. Only when the majority of participants agree on its validity is the transaction permanently recorded. Fig.4.2 illustrates this complete process — from transaction initiation to consensus — demonstrating how the blockchain-based approach ensures system-wide transparency, security, and integrity.

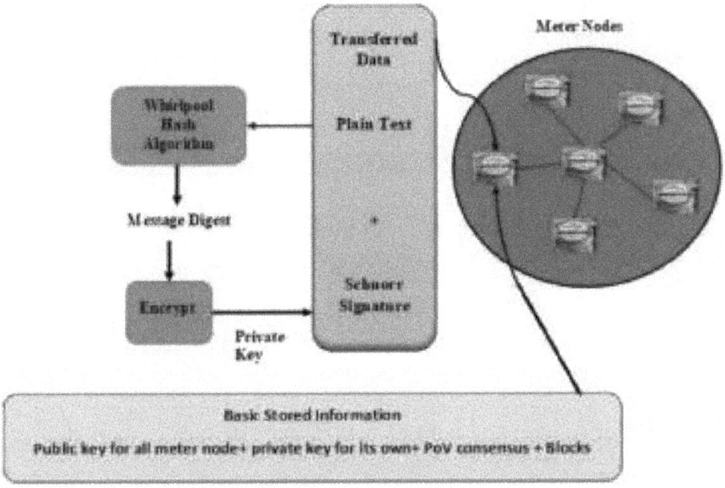

Fig.4.2. Workflow of proposed approach

In a distributed blockchain environment, each cluster is periodically granted the opportunity to validate the accuracy and consistency of its collected data, thereby safeguarding the overall reliability of the network. Achieving consensus is essential to ensure that all participating nodes maintain a synchronized and trustworthy ledger. This agreement is established through a **consensus algorithm** — a predefined set of protocols dictating how nodes confirm the blockchain's current state and validate new entries. To improve both the performance and security of this process, a new mechanism called **E-PoV** (Extended Proof of Vote) is introduced. In this approach, distributed nodes, operated by **Meter nodes**, reach consensus and engage in decentralized arbitration via a structured voting system. E-PoV differentiates between **voting rights** and **accounting responsibilities** while preserving the critical principle that each Meter node maintains a unique, verifiable security identity. This structure guarantees that every node can be individually authenticated, fostering secure and transparent decision-making across the network. Meter nodes are central to this process, performing transaction verification and protecting the blockchain from tampering or inaccuracies.

For efficient data acquisition, transmission, and processing, the proposed system incorporates a **modified Supervisory Control and Data Acquisition (SCADA)** network. While this enhanced SCADA is adapted for blockchain integration, the foundational components of the power distribution infrastructure remain intact. The architecture includes:

- **Data collection modules** at each Meter node, which capture relevant environmental and operational data,
- **Signal transmitters** to relay this data into the network,
- **Signal receivers** enabling node-to-node communication, and
- **Processing units** that handle and analyze incoming data.

Through this design, real-time information is gathered and transmitted across the grid efficiently, while the distributed blockchain framework ensures data integrity, security, and resilience against tampering.

4.3.1. Meter Nodes

In the proposed approach, smart meter nodes are strategically installed on the user's premises to gather a wide range of multidimensional data. This includes crucial information on the user's power consumption, as well as environmental factors such as moisture levels and temperature, which are monitored in real-time. Once a smart meter is deployed, it is assigned a unique identity ID, which is securely stored on the blockchain. This ensures that each meter has a verifiable and tamper-proof record, facilitating secure and transparent tracking of its data and usage. Additionally, whenever the meter is activated, both the meter and its data collection activities are also recorded on the blockchain.

The smart meters are designed to interact with pre-selected reporting nodes, which may vary from round to round. These reporting nodes are responsible for collecting the multidimensional data from the smart meters and transmitting it to the broader network. This design ensures flexibility and scalability, as reporting nodes can be dynamically assigned to handle the flow of data based on system requirements. The smart meter also supports a smart response contract, which is established by the receiver, often integrated with the user's mobile device. This contract enables flexible power control, allowing users to adjust energy usage based on real-time data, enhancing efficiency and reducing costs. Some of the key features of the smart meter nodes are as follows:

Unique Identification: Each meter is distinctly recognized by a unique ID, ensuring that every device can be individually tracked and authenticated within the network.

Cryptographic Capabilities: Each smart meter is equipped with sophisticated software that generates both a public and private key. This cryptographic functionality secures communications and make sure the integrity and authenticity of between the meter and other nodes in the network.

Communication Flexibility: The smart meters are designed to utilize both wired and wireless communication channels, providing adaptability and ensuring reliable data transmission regardless of the network setup or environmental conditions.

Hardware and Data Processing: Each meter is equipped with essential hardware components, including RAM for processing and storing data, a data collection device for capturing real-time readings, computing hardware for processing the data, a signal transmitter for sending data to the network, and a signal receiver for receiving updates from the reporting nodes. This comprehensive setup ensures that the smart meter is capable of efficiently collecting, processing, and communicating data while maintaining the security and privacy of the information.

These features collectively enable the smart meters to function effectively in a distributed blockchain-based system, ensuring secure, real-time data collection and transmission while providing users with greater control over their energy usage.

4.3.2. Data Encryption and Transmission

In the proposed system, each meter node is assigned a unique private and public key pair before entering the data encryption and transmission phase. The public key acts as the node's central, publicly accessible identifier within the network, allowing other nodes to verify its presence and legitimacy. The private key, on the other hand, is used to authenticate the node's actions and ensure that the data it generates or transmits is secure and tamper-proof. This dual-key system forms the foundation of the security framework, ensuring that each node can be uniquely identified and its activities validated through cryptographic methods. Given that the network is decentralized and built on blockchain principles, all data collected by the meter nodes must be securely encoded before transmission to other nodes. This ensures it's really important that sensitive information stays confidential and is kept safe from unauthorised access. The data in each meter node is made up of two main components: basic stored information and transmitted data. The basic stored information includes the public keys of each meter node, the private key for authentication, the pre-established consensus mechanism, and the blocks of data collected by the node. This foundational data structure supports the node's operations and ensures that it can participate in the blockchain system securely. When a meter node collects data, the information is stored in plaintext format initially. Before it is transmitted to the network, this plaintext is encrypted to prevent any interception or tampering. The transmitted data consists of the plaintext (original data) and a digital signature, which is used for verification. To encrypt the data, the Whirlpool hash algorithm is employed to process the plaintext and generate a message digest. This message digest serves as a condensed, irreversible representation of the original data, ensuring its integrity.

Once the message digest is created, the private key is used to encode it, forming Schnorr signature. This cryptographic signature ensures that the message digest has not been altered during transmission. The Schnorr signature is particularly useful because it allows anyone with access to the node's public key to verify the transmitted data, ensuring transparency and trust within the system. To ensure efficiency, the system utilizes **Broadcast Encryption**. Instead of individual encryption for each node O(n), a single ciphertext is broadcast that only authorized nodes with the group key can decrypt O(1). This prevents the "encryption explosion" mentioned. After the encryption and signature generation processes, the transmitted data, including the signature and encrypted message, is sent to all other meter nodes in the network. A decentralised communication model helps make sure that data is safely spread out across the network. Each node that receives the data can check if the transmission is valid by using the sender's public key. This process helps to keep the data safe and also plays a role in ensuring that the whole blockchain system remains trustworthy and clear.

Schnorr Signature Scheme: A Schnorr signature is a type of digital signature used in cryptography. It's considered one of the simplest and most secure ways to verify messages [145]. Named after its creator, Claus Schnorr, the scheme is recognized for its simplicity and strong security guarantees, making it a popular choice for cryptographic communication, especially in blockchain systems and other decentralized networks. In the Schnorr signature process, both the sender and the receiver participate in generating and verifying the digital signature, ensuring the authenticity of the transmitted message. The sender begins by generating a nonce, denoted as r, which is a random value used to ensure the uniqueness and unpredictability of the signature. This nonce is used only once for each message, which helps prevent replay attacks and guarantees that each signature is unique. The next step in the process involves the sender calculating a public key R by multiplying the nonce r with a predefined generator point G on an elliptic curve. The relationship between the nonce and the generator is expressed as $R = r \cdot G$, where R is the public key derived from the sender's private key. This public key R is then shared with the receiver, along with the message that is to be signed. Once the public key R and the message are sent to the receiver, the sender also shares their private key, though the private key itself is not directly transmitted. The private key is used in combination with the message and the nonce to generate the actual signature. The sender and receiver then create a shared task for validation by applying a cryptographic hash function. Specifically, the receiver will hash the combination of the message and the sender's public key R, along with other information, to produce a digest that serves as a unique representation of the message. The sender and receiver can create a shared task for validation by utilizing hashing the mixture of the aforementioned sent information is expressed as,

$$e = H(R\|P\|m) \tag{4.1}$$

After that, the sender figures out that the signature is represented as,

$$s = r + k.e \tag{4.2}$$

Meanwhile, the receiver does not recognize the value of r and K attains $(r + K.e).G = r.G + (K.G).e = R + P.e$. At last, the receiver sends the result $R + P.e$ to the sender for verification purposes, represented as

$$G = R + P.e \tag{4.3}$$

The security of the Schnorr signature system is based on the discrete logarithm assumption, a concept initially proposed by Schnorr. In this context, g represents a generator, and $\mathbb{G}$ is a group with prime order q. The system is defined by three main algorithms: key generation, signing, and verification, each of which plays a critical role in ensuring the integrity and authenticity of the signature.

Key Generation (KeyGen): This procedure takes 1^{λ} as input and outputs a **signing key** sk and a **verification key** vk through the following steps:

- Randomly select $x \overset{\$}{\leftarrow} \mathbb{Z}_q$ and compute $y \leftarrow g^x$
- Define a cryptographic hash function $H: \{0, 1\}^* \rightarrow \mathbb{Z}_q$
- Set $sk = x, vk = (y, H)$.

Signature Generation (Sign): Given a message $m \in \{0, 1\}^*$ and the signing key sk, the signature σ is produced as follows:

- Randomly choose $t \overset{\$}{\leftarrow} \mathbb{Z}_q$ and let $r \leftarrow g^t$
- Compute the hash value $h \leftarrow H(m||r)$ where "||" denotes concatenation.
- Calculate $s \leftarrow x.h + t \bmod q$.
- Output the signature $\sigma \leftarrow (h, s)$.

Signature Verification (Verify): To verify a message m with signature σ using the verification key vk, perform the following:

- Compute $r' \leftarrow g^s y^{-h}$.
- Calculate $h \leftarrow H(m||r)$.
- If $h' = h$, return 1 (valid signature); otherwise, return 0 (invalid signature).

Whirlpool Hash Algorithm: In many cryptographic techniques, the hash function plays a significant role by ensuring data integrity and security. The use of hash functions is fundamental in Blockchain technology, where they are employed to create unique identifiers for data blocks. When a hash function is applied to input data, it produces a fixed-size output, commonly known as a hash or digest, which is almost always unique for each distinct input. This property allows users to verify the integrity of the data, as even a minor change in the input will result in a completely different hash output, indicating any alteration. For example, SHA-256, a widely used hash algorithm, is known for producing a 256-bit output, and its security is based on the computational infeasibility of reversing the hash to retrieve the original data. In proactive reconfigurable computing environments, hash algorithms like SHA-256 are optimized to accelerate their performance, enabling faster verification and secure data transactions, especially in blockchain networks. By utilizing hardware-accelerated approaches, SHA-256 can be implemented more efficiently, providing high throughput while maintaining robust security standards. The whirlpool hash algorithm's design is shown in Fig.4.3.

Whirlpool was selected for its **512-bit hash space**, providing higher collision resistance in high-frequency data environments compared to SHA-256. A comparative analysis of Whirlpool's resistance to length-extension attacks.

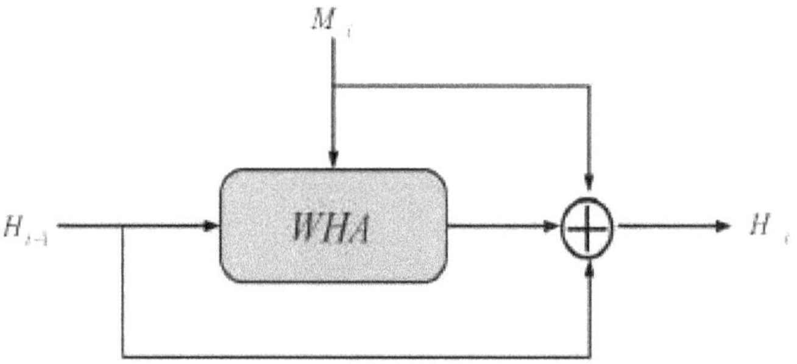

Fig.4.3. Structure of Whirlpool hash algorithm

The WHA is proposed as an effective solution for compressing text within the current block to generate a secure message digest. This algorithm operates as an iterative, one-way hash function, providing robust cryptographic security for a wide range of applications by creating structured message digests with varying dimensions [146]. It can process text inputs of any size up to 2^{256} bits and produces a fixed 512-bit message digest as output, ensuring both consistency and security. When the first meter node in the chain finds a nonce, it sends the value out to all the connected nodes in the network so they can check if it's valid. The verification process is all about checking if the solution meets the set cryptographic requirements, making sure that the data stays secure and unchanged. After that, the address-based distributed voting method is applied to achieve agreement on the validation outcome. Every node in the network gets one chance to verify the trustworthiness and correctness of the information it gets. This decentralised verification method makes sure that data stays intact and builds trust between nodes by stopping manipulation and boosting the overall strength of the blockchain system. The framework becomes really efficient at managing and securing multidimensional data in a decentralised architecture by using Whirlpool.

4.3.3. Data Decryption and validation

All meter routers tasked with collecting transmitted data must decode the information they receive and verify its authenticity. This process ensures that the integrity of the transmitted data is maintained throughout the network. As illustrated in Fig.4.3, the user's key pair is used to decrypt the cipher-text, revealing the second message digest, which is then compared to the first message digest generated by hashing the plaintext received. If the two digests are identical, the data is validated as authentic; however, if they differ, the information is flagged as tampered or invalid. This mechanism helps to safeguard against potential security threats, such as data modification, delays, or deletions, which can compromise the consistency and reliability of the transmitted information. To mitigate such risks, the proposed framework employs a E - PoV consensus mechanism, where each node is granted a single opportunity to evaluate the accuracy and consistency of the incoming data. This consensus process ensures that the decision to accept or reject data is decentralized and collectively determined by multiple nodes in the network. As shown in Fig.4.4, information is only deemed accurate and integrated into the blockchain once a majority of nodes reach a consensus, further strengthening the reliability of the system. By combining cryptographic verification with a robust consensus model, the framework improves security while also ensuring data integrity throughout the whole network.

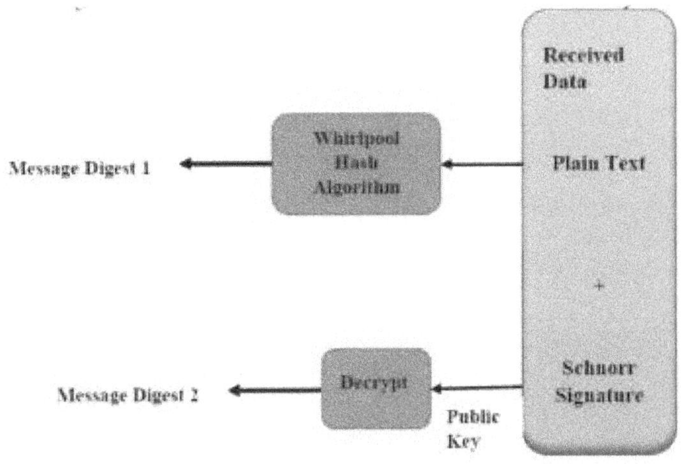

Fig.4.4 Data decryption and validation

The data decryption and validation process, depicted in Fig.4.4, involves critical steps to ensure the accuracy and integrity of the transmitted information. In this process, the received cipher text is decrypted using the recipient's private key, and the resulting plaintext is hashed to generate a message digest. This message digest is compared with the digest derived from the original cipher text to validate the data's authenticity. The consensus process plays a pivotal role in achieving agreement among network nodes, establishing which block candidate should be validated and subsequently added to the blockchain. By employing a distributed approach, the consensus mechanism eliminates reliance on a single point of control, ensuring that all participating nodes contribute to the decision-making process. This collective validation ensures data consistency, prevents unauthorized modifications, and enhances the overall security and transparency of the blockchain network.

Extended -Proof of Vote: In the proposed approach, a novel consensus mechanism called E - PoV has been introduced, enabling distributed nodes, specifically those owned by meter nodes, to achieve consensus and participate in decentralized arbitration through a voting process. PoV uniquely separates voting privileges from accounting responsibilities while maintaining the critical requirement of assigning distinct security identities to each meter node. Unlike traditional third-party intermediaries or unpredictable public input, the PoV mechanism relies on voting outcomes among core consortium members to generate and validate blocks within the blockchain. In this PoV algorithm, the consensus process involves various roles, including commissioners, denoted as $N(C)$, butlers represented as $N(B)$, and butler candidates labeled as $N(BC)$. Additionally, ordinary users are identified by $N(OU)$, with each node capable of assuming multiple roles and fulfilling specific responsibilities within the network. This layered structure ensures that voting and decision-making are secure, transparent, and free from external influence, while maintaining efficiency and scalability in the consensus process.

$$N(All) =\leq N(C) + N(B) + N(BC) + N(OU) \qquad (4.4)$$

Each butler in the system is assigned a unique number ranging from zero to $N(B-1)$. If the number of butler candidates, $N(BC)$, is less than the number of butlers, $N(B)$, the system considers the available terms insufficient for butler candidates. To address this, the system assigns multiple numbers to butlers. For instance, if $N(B)$= 8 and $N(BC)$= 6, the system assigns numbers from 0 to 7 to the butlers, represented as

$$\{B(1), B(2), B(3), B(4), B(5), B(6), B(1), B(2)\} \qquad (4.5)$$

In this scenario, $B(1)$ and $\mathrm{B}(2)$ are designated as the two butlers with the maximum votes, ensuring that they achieve the required butler numbers. Each butler tenure involves generating valid blocks, with the final block in the sequence containing the election results and associated details. A block is deemed valid if it gathers at least $\left\lceil \frac{N(C)}{2} \right\rceil + 1$ signatures from the commissioners. To maintain system efficiency, a servant must produce a legitimate block within the designated packing cycle. As discussed in the previous chapter, the PoV mechanism ensures the consistent generation of blocks, thereby maintaining the integrity and functionality of the blockchain system.

4.4. Results and Discussion

The proposed approach uses the IEEE 118 BUS SYSTEM 118 Bus Model for experiments, which includes 118 nodes, 54 generators, and 186 branches, to assess how resilient SG network systems are to cyber-attacks. Every node has a meter that collects analogue data like current, voltage, and power flow. Meanwhile, each branch is equipped with breakers that gather digital information to check the status of the lines, indicating whether they are open or closed. Also, there are two meters set up at each end of every line in every branch to keep track of analogue data like power flows, voltage, and current. The methodology is tested against cyber-attacks under two scenarios. In the first scenario, 676 sensors (comprising 118 nodes, 186 branches, and two meters per branch) collect necessary data from remote locations, resulting in 676 communication channels connecting the sensors to the central controller. In the second scenario, the same 676 sensors are considered, but the communication network among them includes 676 × (676-1)/2 = 228,150 interaction channels. This evaluation accounts for the uncertainty in the likelihood of cyber attackers successfully infiltrating devices, stealing critical data, compromising communication channels, or altering substantial amounts of information within the network.

Table 4.1. Comparison of consensus algorithm

Consensus Algorithm	Security	Resource consumption	Transaction confirmation time	Transaction throughput
PoW	High	High	Long	Small

PoS	Little high	Medium	Medium	Small
PoV	High	Low	Short	High

Table 4.1 highlights a comparative analysis of recent consensus algorithms [147], demonstrating that the proposed PoV consensus mechanism offers notable advantages in terms of security, resource efficiency, transaction confirmation time, and transaction throughput. Traditional consensus methods, such as PoW, rely on cryptographic evidence where one entity proves to another that a significant amount of computational effort has been expended. While secure, PoW suffers from inefficiencies, including long transaction confirmation times and low throughput, making it not the best fit for applications that require real-time processing or have limited resources. Conversely, PoS algorithms select verifiers based on their stake in the associated cryptocurrency. While PoS improves efficiency compared to PoW, it still falls short in achieving stable resource consumption and offers only medium security, moderate transaction confirmation times, and limited throughput. These limitations hinder its performance in scenarios requiring high scalability and robust security, such as power grids or blockchain-based critical infrastructures. To address these challenges, the proposed PoV consensus mechanism introduces a voting-based approach wherein distributed nodes, managed by meter nodes, participate in decentralized arbitration. This voting system ensures enhanced performance by improving security, reducing resource consumption variability, and enabling faster transaction confirmation with higher throughput. PoV is particularly effective in mitigating cyber-attacks by leveraging its decentralized nature and cryptographic underpinnings to enhance data integrity and system reliability.

The proposed E-PoV consensus framework, integrated with statistical modeling, demonstrates strong resilience and performance under diverse operational and attack conditions. Probability Mass Function (PMF) and Cumulative Distribution Function (CDF) analyses confirm the system's robustness in handling probabilistic events, validating its reliability and security trade-offs.

Chi-square and non-central chi-square CDF evaluations reveal that higher λ values improve outcome predictability, while attack simulations—such as the 51% attack scenario—highlight potential vulnerabilities and the necessity of layered cybersecurity defenses. Without reputation mechanisms, false event rates remain measurable; however, incorporating Reputation Score significantly reduces incorrect occurrences, prioritizes trustworthy nodes, and strengthens error mitigation.

Comparative success rate analysis across varying attacker densities confirms that the proposed approach maintains high operational integrity, even under increased adversarial influence. Scalability tests, examining throughput and latency against relay count, show that the modular architecture supports efficient load distribution, mitigates bottlenecks, and sustains optimal communication performance under high relay density.

Overall, results verify that the E-PoV consensus, combined with blockchain integration, offers a secure, scalable, and attack-resilient framework for modern power grid operations.

4.5.Summary

Blockchain technology has gained considerable attention from researchers across multiple domains, particularly for enhancing cyber security in Smart Grids (SG). When applied in this context, blockchain functions as a strong defensive barrier, preventing malicious actors from altering critical data. Although numerous studies have explored blockchain-enabled SG solutions, limited research has directly addressed the critical issue of the 51% attack scenario where an adversary gains control over the majority of network nodes, enabling the creation of a fraudulent consensus on voting outcomes. While executing such an attack on a large public network is highly challenging, it remains a significant concern for blockchain-based systems.

To counter this, the present work introduces a Novel Distributed Blockchain-Based Protection Architecture aimed at strengthening the self-defence capabilities of modern power systems against cyber threats. Within the proposed framework, all collected data is securely stored as linked blocks in a decentralized ledger, with each block cryptographically bound to the previous one. These records are distributed across meter nodes, ensuring no single point of failure. Data packets contain both plaintext and cryptographic signatures, with the Schnorr Signature scheme providing secure authentication. For hashing, the Whirlpool algorithm—an iterative, one-way cryptographic function capable of processing inputs of up to 2^{256} bits and producing a fixed 512-bit digest—is employed to ensure message integrity.

Furthermore, a novel consensus mechanism named E-PoV is proposed, where distributed meter nodes participate in consensus formation and decentralized arbitration through a structured voting process. This method distinctly separates voting rights from accounting responsibilities while preserving unique, verifiable security identities for all meter nodes. By leveraging this approach, the proposed blockchain framework significantly enhances the resilience, reliability, and cyber security of power grid operations.

4.6. Conclusion

The suggested method presents a new, distributed blockchain-based protection system aimed at improving the self-defence abilities of current power systems against cyberattacks by utilising the distributed security aspects of blockchain technology. This new cybersecurity solution presents a fresh approach to securing power systems. It includes important technological insights, along with an assessment of advancements, comparisons, and the challenges of implementing blockchain technology. This study looks at how well this strategy works in stopping cyberattacks, showing that the E-PoV consensus blockchain might be a good option for keeping data safe in current power systems. The system's performance has been assessed based on possible threat scenarios and has shown to be successful. The suggested blockchain technology has the potential to greatly enhance the security and resilience of power grids by using meters as nodes in a distributed network, with meter data being encoded into blocks. Using E - PoV in the distributed blockchain really boosts the system's defence against cyberattacks. In the future, I plan to work on improving the performance of the blockchain system using E - PoV. The goal is to find a balance between protecting privacy and meeting regulatory requirements, while also making it more secure against cyberattacks. The proposed system has some cool benefits, like using fewer resources, confirming transactions really quickly, and providing better security and throughput when you compare it to the consensus algorithms we have now. In future developments, the right version of blockchain technology will be used in public sector projects to enhance the privacy and confidentiality of people's data.

CHAPTER 5

BLOCKCHAIN-ENABLED CYBER DEFENSE IN MODERN POWER SYSTEMS: THE GRID-LOCK APPROACH

5.1. Introduction

Blockchain technology has garnered significant attention across various domains, particularly for its potential to revolutionize cybersecurity in power grids. As modern power systems become increasingly reliant on digital frameworks, they are exposed to sophisticated cyber threats that challenge the resilience and reliability of critical infrastructures. One area of concern is the vulnerability of community identity servers in power grid, which can jeopardize grid stability and delay real-time operations. To address these challenges, this chapter introduces a novel framework called the Grid-Lock Secure-chain Consensus Framework. This innovative approach leverages blockchain technology to enhance the cybersecurity and operational efficiency of modern power systems. At the core of this framework the E-PoV consensus mechanism, which enables decentralized voting among meter nodes to achieve secure consensus. Each meter node is equipped with public and private keys to ensure safe identification and transaction validation. All transmitted data is encrypted and stored on a distributed ledger, with blocks cryptographically linked using the WHA algorithm. The E-PoV mechanism guarantees that only valid blocks are incorporated into the blockchain, while preserving separate voting and accounting privileges to bolster system security. The proposed architecture focuses on enhancing encryption methods and decentralizing permission control, thereby minimizing the likelihood of cyber intrusions without hindering operational efficiency. By embedding blockchain within the system, this strategy not only fortifies the grid against emerging threats but also improves its robustness and functional performance. A comprehensive evaluation conducted on the IEEE 118-Bus System configuration highlights notable improvements in both throughput and latency when compared to conventional approaches. This novel framework represents a significant leap forward in leveraging blockchain for safeguarding modern power infrastructure.

5.2. Proposed methodology

The cybersecurity of advanced power systems has become a critical focus in research and industry, prompting the development of robust mechanisms to detect and mitigate cyberattacks. However, existing frameworks face significant challenges, including vulnerabilities in the community identification server within smart power grid. These vulnerabilities may lead to cyberattacks and errors in detection. Additionally, the complexities of blockchain technology, decentralized authorization, and encryption can increase computational overhead and resource consumption, potentially slow real-time operations and impacting overall system performance. While an increase in miners can reduce mining time, consensus mechanisms often involve trade-offs, such as increased difficulty levels, which further complicate these systems.

To address these challenges, this research proposes a Grid-Lock Secure-chain Consensus Framework designed to enhance the resilience of modern power systems against cyberattacks. In this framework, each meter node within the network is assigned unique public and private keys, enabling secure identification and action validation. All information collected by meter nodes is encrypted before transmission and stored in a distributed ledger as linked units across the storage spaces of individual meters. The framework utilizes the WHA algorithm to cryptographically link blocks, ensuring data integrity and security within the distributed blockchain network. To validate and approve new blocks, a novel consensus mechanism called E-PoV is introduced. E-PoV facilitates decentralized arbitration by enabling distributed meter nodes to achieve consensus through a voting process. This mechanism separates voting and accounting privileges, assigning distinct security identities to meter nodes while ensuring that only legitimate blocks are added to the blockchain. Core consortium members participate in the voting process to determine which E-PoV blocks are generated and verified. Each meter node encrypts its message digest using its private key to create a signature, which is then shared across the network. Other nodes verify and decode this information to ensure authenticity and validity.

By leveraging meter nodes as part of a distributed system, the proposed blockchain framework enhances the safety and reliability of power systems. It encodes meter data into secure blocks, significantly improving system resilience against cyber threats. Fig.5.1 presents a block diagram of the proposed framework, offering an overview of its components and processes. Further discussion on the blockchain network implementation follows in subsequent sections.

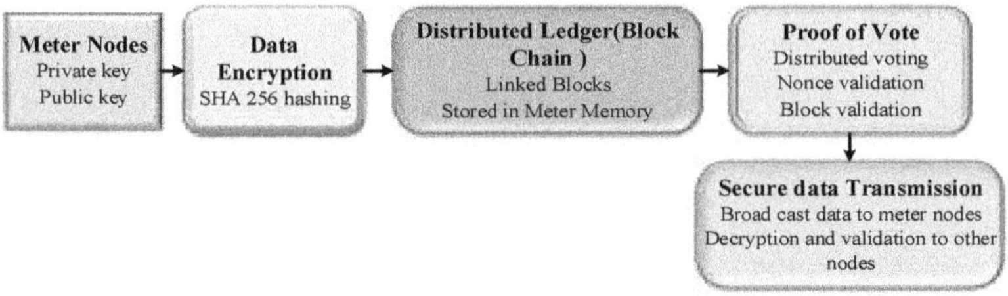

Fig.5.1. Block schematic illustrating the proposed approach

5.2.1. Blockchain Network

Blockchain is the name of a technology that uses an ever-growing collection of data structures called blocks, linked together in a secure and immutable manner. Cryptography plays a crucial role in connecting and safeguarding these blocks, ensuring the integrity, confidentiality, and authenticity of the data they contain. The technology relies on a highly sophisticated encryption system that facilitates secure data transmission across decentralized networks. Similar to a business ledger, Blockchain meticulously records every peer-to-peer transaction, creating a transparent and trustworthy digital log. Each block contains essential information, including a timestamp, transaction details, and the unique identifier of the block that precedes it. These blocks are interconnected, forming a chain that ensures historical accuracy and traceability. Once data within a block is validated and approved by the network participants, it becomes immutable, ensuring that tampering or unauthorized alterations are effectively prevented. Blockchain technology is specifically designed to combat data manipulation and fraud by embedding trust and transparency into its architecture. Each block in the chain houses critical information, as depicted in Fig.5.2. This includes the current block value, execution time of transactions, address of the previous block, a random number known as a nonce, and the current block header. Together, these components form the core structure that stores both the quantity and specifics of the data collected. Additionally, Blockchain ensures the perpetual availability and permanence of stored data, making it highly reliable for various applications. To enhance security and authenticity, the data is protected using digital signatures based on cryptographic constructs like Merkle trees. These digital signatures ensure that the data is unreplicable and verify its integrity. The Merkle-tree hash function processes the received data, creating a unique Merkle-root value that remains consistent and distinctive for each block. This innovative approach not only strengthens data security but also enables efficient verification processes within the Blockchain framework.

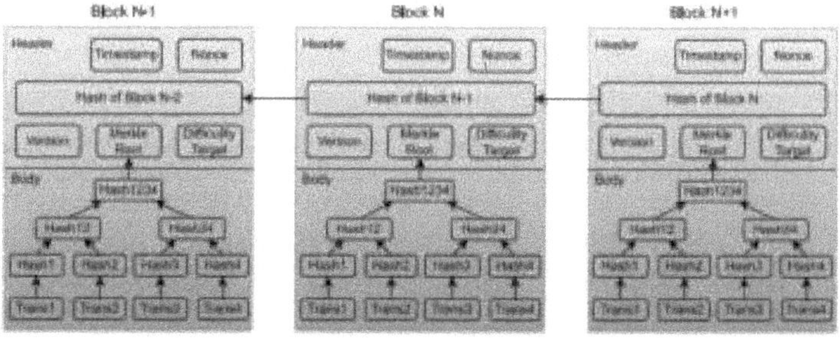

Fig.5.2. Blockchain structure and Merkle hash tree

The information contained within each block varies depending on the type of blockchain. Each block is uniquely identified by a hash code, which acts as a digital fingerprint. This hash code updates whenever the block's contents are altered. The inclusion of the previous block's hash, serving as its identifier, ensures the creation of a continuous chain. Since any change to one block disrupts the integrity of subsequent blocks, the blockchain remains highly interconnected and resistant to tampering. Blockchain technology can be viewed as a specialized form of ledger technology that records transactional data, functioning much like a digital notepad. This "notepad" is organized into a sequence of blocks, which grows as new entries are added. Each time new data is recorded, a new block is generated and securely linked to the preceding blocks using unique hash codes. This process creates an immutable and secure chain of records. The first block serves as the foundational link, while subsequent blocks act as connected entries. Any attempt to modify the contents of a block disrupts the links to the subsequent blocks due to changes in the block's hash code. This ensures that alterations to the data are immediately detectable, preserving the blockchain's integrity.

To further secure the blockchain, consensus algorithms play a critical role. One such algorithm, introduced in this research, is the E-PoV method, a novel approach that enables distributed nodes, referred to as Meter nodes, to reach consensus and engage in voting-based decentralized arbitration. E-PoV emphasizes the importance of assigning unique security identities to Meter nodes while differentiating between voting rights and accounting privileges. Unlike systems that rely on high public awareness or third-party intermediaries, the E-PoV method leverages votes cast by core consortium members to generate and validate blocks. This ensures a secure, efficient, and decentralized decision-making process.

The Whirlpool Hash Algorithm, commonly referred to as WHA-256, is a widely used cryptographic technique that generates a fixed-length hash output of 256 bits, equivalent to 32 bytes. This algorithm is designed to create a unique digital fingerprint for any given piece of data, such as a file or a message. The process involves applying a highly sophisticated mathematical operation to the input data, resulting in a distinct output value known as a hash. This hash serves as a digital representation or fingerprint of the original input, ensuring the data's authenticity and integrity. WHA is extensively employed in various applications, including digital signatures, password authentication systems, and blockchain technology. By leveraging the cryptographic hash function, any text or data can be transformed into a unique 256-bit alphanumeric string, referred to as a hash value. This transformation ensures that even the slightest change to the input data produces a completely different hash, highlighting the algorithm's sensitivity to data modifications.

A key feature of WHA is its collision resistance, which ensures that no two distinct inputs can produce the same hash output. This property is crucial for maintaining the algorithm's reliability, as it prevents attackers from generating duplicate hashes for different data sets. The primary objective of WHA is to guarantee data security by making collisions computationally infeasible, thereby safeguarding the uniqueness of each hash. Moreover, WHA plays a pivotal role in blockchain technology, where it ensures the immutability and security of blocks by generating unique identifiers for each. It is also utilized in digital signatures to verify the authenticity of electronic documents and in password authentication systems to securely store and validate credentials. By combining efficiency, security, and robustness, WHA has become a cornerstone of modern cryptographic practices.

5.2.2 Block Creation

A consensus round is executed in multiple packing cycles. If the designated butler fails to generate a valid block within the allotted time, authority is transferred to the servant to complete block creation. The overall duration of a consensus round implies that any invalid blocks encountered during the process are discarded. The following steps outline the creation of a valid block:

- **User interaction**: Regular users initiate transactions and sign them. These transactions are verified for legitimacy before being forwarded to commissioners and servants.
- **Butler operations**: Butlers record verified transactions in their local pool. All butlers and commissioners maintain synchronized NTP (Network Time Protocol) clocks for consistency.
- **Tenure considerations**: If the block is the first in a tenure, the preceding block is treated as the last valid special block of the previous term. For a genesis block, the value of R is set to zero.
- **Pre-block preparation**: The duty butler collects transactions from the local pool, compiles them into a pre-block, and shares it with commissioners. A cutoff timestamp is assigned.
- **Commissioner validation**: Upon receiving the pre-block, commissioners verify its legitimacy, sign it, and return their signatures with a current timestamp to the butler.
- **Signature aggregation**: The duty butler collects signatures from commissioners, arranges them in ascending timestamp order, and adds this sequence to the pre-header.
- **Header finalization**: The R-value is calculated, and the block time is set to the latest timestamp received. If the timestamp is earlier than the cutoff, the pre-

header is updated with the required signatures. Otherwise, the block becomes invalid and is discarded.

- **Block confirmation**: The finalized block is distributed to all commissioners and then to the network. Once more than 50% of commissioners acknowledge receipt, the block is officially confirmed and added to the chain.
- **Next round initiation**: Upon acceptance, assistants and officials extract transactions from their public pools, determine the next random number *R*, and begin the subsequent consensus round.

The final block in a tenure triggers the election of the next butler team:

P_1 – The duty butler receives a candidate list from the commissioners, combining both current and aspiring butlers, to prepare a voting process.

P_2 – Votes are submitted by commissioners and current butlers, then stored in the local pool.

P_3 – If votes exceed half of the total commissioners, the process continues with P_4–P_8 to produce a special block. Otherwise, the election is delayed until the set expiration time.

P_4–P_8 – Similar to regular block generation (S_4–S_8), special blocks require commissioner signatures but include only voting transactions. The top N_b nodes from the election become the new butlers for the upcoming tenure.

P_9 – Once the special block is generated, current butlers are relieved of duty, and related voting transactions are cleared from the local pool.

Genesis Block Creation

The genesis block, with a height of zero, is unique to the consortium blockchain. It contains initial details about the first set of butler nodes and consortium members, forming the foundation for future blocks:

T_1 – Primary commissioner nodes verify online availability by exchanging messages. Each node has an address hash, and the commissioner with the smallest hash acts as the proxy.

T_2 – The primary commissioner sends an update transaction to the proxy commissioner.

T_3 – Commissioners applying for butler positions submit identity change requests, which are stored locally.

T_4 – From the candidate list, commissioners select at least *K* butler addresses, serialize them into a vote, sign it, and forward it to the proxy commissioner.

T_5 – The proxy commissioner compiles all transactions into a pre-block and sends it to all commissioners. Once all signatures are collected, the genesis block is finalized, confirming network establishment.

T_6 – Upon receipt of the genesis block, any unconfirmed local transactions are removed.

5.2.3 Random Number Generation

To fairly select the next duty butler, each block generates a random number *R*. The process is as follows:

- The duty butler collects signatures and timestamps from *K* commissioners, represented as

$$\langle \text{C-time}(i), \text{C-sign}(i) \rangle, \tag{5.1}$$

  where $0 \leq i < K$ and $\lfloor N(c)/2 \rfloor < K \leq N(c)$.

- Entries are sorted in ascending order of C-time, with C-time(K–1) being the largest.
- A seed value is generated:

$$R\_sor = \text{C-time}(K-1) \oplus \text{C-sign}(K-1) \tag{5.2}$$

- The final 32 bits of the hash of R_sor are extracted, converted to an integer, and reduced modulo N_b to obtain:

$$R = StrToInt(SubstringEnd32(Hash(R\_sor))) \bmod N\_b \qquad (5.3)$$

- Because R_sor and R are unique for each block, the method prevents collusion by ensuring that participants cannot manipulate values to influence the butler selection sequence.

5.3. Results and discussion

The outcome, performance analysis, comparison, and discussion section evaluate the efficiency and effectiveness of the proposed approach in detail. By implementing a consensus mechanism based on E-PoV, the approach successfully created a functional smart contract, which was rigorously tested on the Ethereum network to assess its real-world applicability. The performance was benchmarked against traditional consensus mechanisms to highlight E-PoV's advantages in terms of transaction speed, scalability, and security. Furthermore, the results showed that the E-PoV-based smart contract outperformed existing systems in terms of reduced latency and improved block generation consistency. These findings underscore the potential of E-PoV in enhancing blockchain network performance while maintaining decentralization and trust.

5.3.1. Experimental setup

The implementation of the proposed method utilizes a system configuration featuring 16GB RAM, a 64-bit operating system, and an Intel Core i5-6200U processor, providing adequate computational capacity to support consensus-driven operations in the blockchain setup. This configuration supports the efficient execution and verification of transactions, which are crucial for maintaining the integrity of the blockchain network. The blockchain's role in improving security is particularly evident in its potential to mitigate vulnerabilities present in traditional SCADA systems. The empirical evaluation, carried out across IEEE 118 BUS SYSTEM 118-bus model, demonstrates how blockchain can bolster the resilience of SG network systems against cyber-attacks. This work leverages the IEEE 118

BUS SYSTEM 118-bus model to simulate the power grids operation and evaluates its performance in the face of potential security threats.

The system is composed of essential elements such as transmission lines, generators, loads, and capacitor banks. Each node is equipped with a meter to record key analog parameters like current, voltage, and power flow, supporting real-time monitoring and operational decisions. Circuit breakers are installed along each branch to gather digital status data, indicating whether a line is active or disconnected. Furthermore, two meters are positioned at both ends of every line to capture a combination of analog and digital information, including voltage, current, and power flow metrics. These measurements play a crucial role in continuously assessing the network's operational health. Fig.5.3 illustrates the IEEE 118-bus model, detailing the placement of components, meters, and branches for comprehensive data collection and transmission. This configuration enables rapid detection of faults and irregularities, thereby strengthening grid management strategies and improving resilience against cyber threats. The integration of blockchain technology further enhances system security by ensuring data integrity and enabling tamper-resistant transaction records within power grid operations.

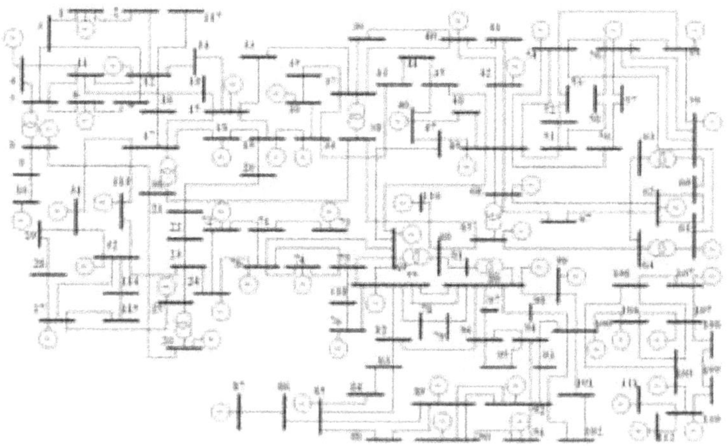

Fig.5.3 IEEE 118 BUS SYSTEM 118 bus model

5.3.2. Performance Analysis

The proposed E-PoV-based blockchain framework was evaluated on the IEEE 118 BUS SYSTEM 118-bus model to assess its performance in secure, decentralized decision-making for SG networks. Block mining time was used as the primary performance metric, revealing an initial uniform mining duration for the first four blocks, followed by a gradual increase and a sharp rise from block 9 onward, peaking at ~1091 ms by block 12. This reflects the cumulative computational load and consensus complexity as the blockchain grows, demonstrating the EPoV mechanism's balance between security and efficiency.

Throughput analysis showed steady improvement with transaction load, reaching ~130 TPS at 150 relay transactions/sec and plateauing near 160 TPS at higher loads, indicating effective scalability up to the system's capacity limits. Latency performance improved significantly, dropping from 0.91 s to ~0.2 s as transaction rates increased, highlighting PoV's capability to expedite consensus and maintain responsiveness under higher loads.

Overall, the results confirm that the PoV consensus mechanism enhances security, scalability, and operational efficiency in blockchain-enabled SG systems, with potential for further optimization to handle extreme transaction volumes.

Latency in our experiments was calculated as End-to-End (E2E) Transaction Latency. This is defined as the time elapsed from the moment a transaction is submitted to the network T_{submit} to the moment it is confirmed in a block $T_{confirm}$:

$$L = T_{confirm} - T_{submit}$$

To ensure statistical significance, we measured:

Propagation Latency: Time taken for the transaction to reach a majority of nodes

Consensus Latency: Time required for the PoV mechanism to reach agreement.

Average Throughput Correlation: Latency was monitored under varying workloads (100 to 1000 Transactions Per Second) to observe the "saturation point" of the network.

Table 5.1. Performance comparison of the proposed method with existing method

Consensus Mechanism	Throughput (Tx/s)	Latency(s)
PBFT without IEEE 118 BUS SYSTEM bus	98	11
PoW without IEEE 118 BUS SYSTEM bus	120	1
EPoV with IEEE 118 BUS SYSTEM bus	150	0.89

Table 5.1 compares the performance of three consensus mechanisms—PBFT, PoW, and the proposed EPoV—within the IEEE 118-bus system model. The assessment focuses on throughput (transactions per second, Tx/s) and latency (seconds) for each approach, independent of the specific bus model characteristics. Findings indicate that EPoV delivers a clear performance advantage, achieving 150 Tx/s with a latency of 0.89 seconds. In contrast, PBFT records 98 Tx/s with 11 seconds latency, while PoW reaches 120 Tx/s with a 1-second delay. This marked improvement in both speed and responsiveness demonstrates PoV's efficiency, especially for power grid applications where rapid data handling is crucial for ensuring operational security and stability. The notably lower latency allows transactions to be validated almost in real time, supporting faster detection and mitigation of cyber threats. Overall, the results underscore EPoV's superior throughput and latency performance compared to conventional consensus methods such as PBFT and PoW. This makes PoV particularly suitable for environments like the IEEE 118 BUS SYSTEM bus model, where fast and efficient transaction processing is vital for system reliability and security. The significant improvement in throughput and latency suggests that PoV could be a highly effective solution for blockchain-based power grid systems, offering enhanced real-time data processing and better handling of high transaction volumes.

5.4. Summary

The PoV consensus method presents an innovative solution that addresses the inherent trade-offs typically faced by other consensus mechanisms, such as low latency versus high throughput. Traditional consensus mechanisms like PBFT and PoW have their own limitations when applied to systems requiring both high efficiency and reliability. PBFT, while providing fault tolerance, suffers from high latency, making it ill-suited for applications that require rapid reaction times. The delay in PBFT's decision-making process can hinder real-time operations, particularly in systems like power grids where swift data processing and quick decision-making are critical. On the other hand, PoW, although it reduces latency, comes at the expense of significant energy consumption and processing resources. This high computational cost and energy usage can be prohibitively expensive, especially in large-scale systems like the IEEE 118 BUS SYSTEM 118 bus model, where efficiency and scalability are paramount. In contrast, the PoV consensus mechanism effectively addresses these challenges by blending the strengths of both PBFT and PoW, while minimizing their respective drawbacks. PoV achieves low latency and high throughput by incorporating a voting-based consensus architecture that optimizes transaction processing times. This approach reduces the computational cost and energy requirements compared to PoW, making it a more sustainable option for large-scale systems. At the same time, PoV retains the key advantages of fast transaction verification and enhanced security, which are essential for power grid applications. Its ability to handle high transaction volumes quickly and efficiently makes it an ideal candidate for environments like the IEEE 118 BUS SYSTEM 118 bus model, where the need for real-time processing is critical for ensuring system stability and security. In summary, the PoV consensus method offers a more balanced and efficient alternative to traditional consensus algorithms like PBFT and PoW, especially in the context of power grid networks. By improving both throughput and latency while reducing energy consumption, PoV provides a scalable, cost-effective, and secure solution to the challenges faced by conventional blockchain-based systems. Its ability to handle large transaction volumes and its applicability to real-time applications such as cyberattack prevention make it a superior choice for the protection and optimization of power grid infrastructure.

5.5. Conclusion

The claim of 51% resistance is based on the Hybridization Factor. Because an attacker must simultaneously possess 51% of the network's hashing power (PoW) and 51% of the voting stake (PoV), the cost of the attack is significantly higher than in a single-mechanism chain.

The proposed **Grid-Lock Secure-Chain Consensus Framework**, integrating the EPoV consensus mechanism, demonstrates significant potential in enhancing the cybersecurity posture of modern power grids. By enabling decentralized voting among meter nodes, supported by robust cryptographic measures such as public–private key pairs, strong encryption, and WHA based distributed ledger protection, the framework ensures both data integrity and transparency in the consensus process. The strategic separation of accounting and voting rights further fortifies the system against unauthorized modifications, reducing the risk of cyberattacks while preserving operational efficiency.

Empirical evaluation on the IEEE 118-bus system confirms the framework's superior performance in terms of throughput and latency compared to conventional methods, highlighting its capability to maintain resilience under dynamic network conditions. These findings indicate that the framework is well-suited for real-time, security-critical power grid applications.

Future work will focus on incorporating adaptive algorithms to optimize performance in complex and evolving grid environments, as well as evaluating scalability for large-scale deployments. Overall, the Grid-Lock Secure-Chain Consensus Framework offers a promising pathway toward establishing a new standard for secure, efficient, and resilient smart grid operations.

CHAPTER 6

RESULT AND DISCUSSION

6.1. Introduction

The success of the proposed approach is thoroughly examined in the Results and Discussion section, where various metrics and performance indicators are evaluated to assess its effectiveness. The implementation of the proposed technique is executed using the Python framework, which provides a versatile and powerful environment for developing machine learning and signal processing applications. The system configuration for the suggested solution is designed to optimize performance and ensure smooth operation. It is built on a 64-bit operating system, enabling efficient handling of large datasets and execution of complex computations often required in signal processing tasks. To support the demanding requirements of the proposed method, the system is equipped with 16.0 GB of RAM. Overall, this configuration is specifically tailored to meet the technical demands of the proposed approach, ensuring that the system operates effectively in various scenarios.

6.2. E-PoV Consensus Framework for fifty one percent Attack Resilience in Power Grids

In the proposed approach, the IEEE 118 BUS SYSTEM is utilized for experimental purposes, consisting of 118 nodes, 54 generators, and 186 branches. This study applies the IEEE 118 BUS SYSTEM to evaluate the resilience of power grids network systems against cyber-attacks. Every node has a meter that collects analogue data like current, voltage, and power flow. Additionally, each branch is equipped with breakers that gather digital information to check the status of the lines, indicating whether they are open or closed. Also, there are two meters set up at each end of every line in every branch to keep track of analogue data like power flows, voltage, and current. The methodology is tested against cyber-attacks under two scenarios. In the first scenario, 676 sensors (comprising 118 nodes, 186 branches, and two meters per branch) collect necessary data from remote locations, resulting in 676 communication channels connecting the sensors to the central controller. In the second scenario, the same 676 sensors are considered, but the communication network among them includes 676 × (676-1)/2 = 228,150 interaction channels. This evaluation accounts for the uncertainty in the likelihood of cyber attackers successfully infiltrating devices, stealing critical data, compromising communication channels, or altering substantial amounts of information within the network.

Table 6.1. Comparison of consensus algorithm

Consensus Algorithm	Security	Resource consumption	Transaction confirmation time	Transaction throughput
Proof of Work (PoW)	High	High	Long	Small
Proof of Stakes (PoS)	Little high	Medium	Medium	Small
Proof of Vote (PoV)	High	Low	Short	High

Table 6.1 highlights a comparative analysis of recent consensus algorithms [147], demonstrating that the proposed EPoV consensus mechanism offers notable advantages in terms of security, resource efficiency, transaction confirmation time, and transaction throughput. Traditional consensus methods, such as PoW, rely on cryptographic evidence where one entity proves to another that a significant amount of computational effort has been expended. While secure, PoW suffers from inefficiencies, including long transaction confirmation times and low throughput, making it Less ideal for real-time or resource-limited environments, whereas PoS algorithms choose validators according to the amount of stake they hold in the linked cryptocurrency. While PoS improves efficiency compared to PoW, it still falls short in achieving stable resource consumption and offers only medium security, moderate transaction confirmation times, and limited throughput. These limitations hinder its performance in scenarios requiring high scalability and robust security, such as power grids or blockchain-based critical infrastructures. To address these challenges, the proposed E-PoV consensus mechanism introduces a voting-based approach wherein distributed nodes, managed by meter nodes,

participate in decentralized arbitration. This voting system ensures enhanced performance by improving security, reducing resource consumption variability, and enabling faster transaction confirmation with higher throughput. E- PoV is particularly effective in mitigating cyber-attacks by leveraging its decentralized nature and cryptographic underpinnings to enhance data integrity and system reliability.

Probability of mass function (PMF)

The examination of the cumulative distribution function (CDF) using chi-square transmission and non-central chi-square dispersion provides valuable insights into the behavior of random variables in statistical modeling. In this context, the probability mass function (PMF) (Fig. 6.1) plays a crucial role by quantifying the likelihood that a discrete random variable ($\boldsymbol{X}$) takes on a specific value within its sample space. This PMF is an essential tool for understanding the distribution of discrete random variables, as it provides a clear representation of the probabilities associated with each possible outcome.

Furthermore, the cumulative distribution curve derived from the PMF serves to explain the response variable's probability density function (PDF). The CDF provides a comprehensive view of the probability that the random variable will take on a value less than or equal to a specified threshold. This is particularly useful for interpreting the probabilities associated with discrete, continuous, or mixed parameters. Incorporating the probability density function alongside the CDF enables the determination of total probability for a random variable. The PDF effectively summarizes the likelihood of different outcomes occurring over a continuous range, thereby facilitating a deeper understanding of the variable's distribution. Overall, this comprehensive analysis of the PMF and the associated cumulative distribution functions provides a robust framework for evaluating the probabilities and behaviors of random variables, which can be applied across various fields of study.

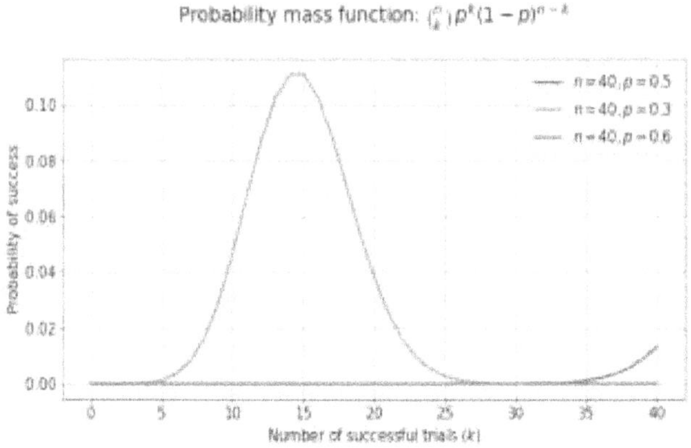

Fig.6.1. Probability Mass Function

Fig.6.2 shows the cumulative distribution function (CDF) of the chi-square distribution. The chi-square test is a common statistical method used to look at the relationship between categorical variables or columns in a dataset. This shows how strongly these variables are related to each other, without taking into account the order of the data. This test is really helpful for figuring out if the data we see is different from what we expected based on a certain hypothesis. To carry out a chi-square test properly, there are a few steps that need to be taken:

Explain what hypotheses are: Begin by explicitly stating the null hypothesis (H_0) and the alternative hypothesis (H_1). The null hypothesis typically asserts that no relationship exists between the variables, while the alternative hypothesis suggests the presence of a relationship.

Figure out the alpha level: Determine the significance level () according to the acceptable margin of error relevant to your field. If α=0.05, that means there's a 5% chance of rejecting H0 when it's true, which relates to a 95% confidence level.

Clean Data: Check the dataset for inconsistencies, such as missing values (NaNs) or other anomalies, to ensure the accuracy of the analysis.

Verify Assumptions: Confirm that the data meets the test's assumptions, such as independence of observations and a sufficient sample size.

Conduct the Test: Use the chi-square test to calculate the test statistic and the p-value.

Make Inferences: Look at the p-value and see how it stacks up against the significance level you've picked. If the p-value is lower than α, We dismiss the null hypothesis, confirming a significant association between the variables. If not, we can't reject H0, which means there's not enough evidence to show a relationship exists. This process helps us figure out if the data we see matches what we expected, which is why the chi-square test is such an important tool in testing hypotheses and analysing categorical data. The method for the Chi-square test is outlined below:

$$x^2 = \sum \frac{(O_i - E_i)^2}{E_i} \tag{6.2}$$

Where, x^2= chi square, O_i= observed value, E_i=expected value.

The Chi-square equation serves as a research tool for analyzing multiple data elements. It is denoted by x^2 and is used for data with attributes distributed across different categories.

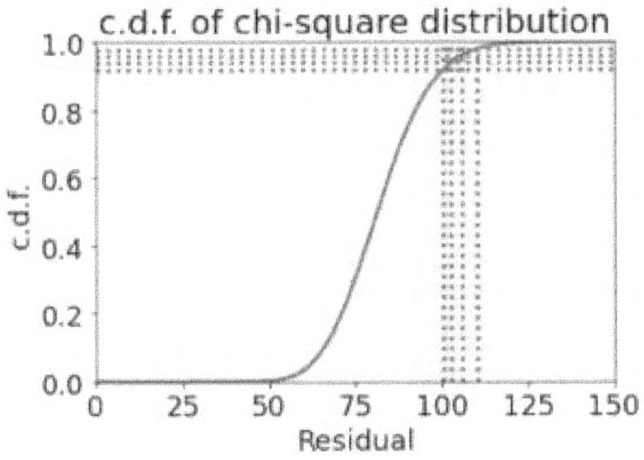

Fig.6.2 CDF of chi-square distribution

Fig.6.3 illustrates the CDF of the non-central chi-square distribution. By examining different values of λ, such as 0, 20, 40, 60, and 80, we can observe how the probability distribution changes under various conditions. As λ increases, the chances of a butler winning the election also rise, indicating that the likelihood of receiving votes grows with higher λ values. This suggests that a higher value of λ corresponds to stronger evidence supporting a particular outcome, thereby increasing the probability that the butler will gain sufficient votes to be elected. Consequently, the election process becomes more predictable as λ becomes larger, as the butler's chances of securing votes improve in these scenarios.

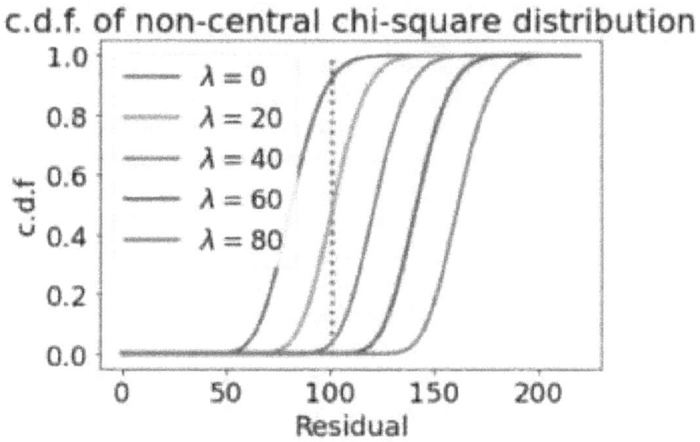

Fig.6.3 CDF of non-central Chi-square distribution

Fig.6.4 illustrates the CDF of Chi-square distribution attack for the proposed approach. A fifty one percent attack is when someone takes control of more than half of the mining power in a blockchain network, which can lead to some serious issues. With this overwhelming control, the attacker can delay the verification and sequencing of new transactions. This can lead to disruptions in the network's normal operations, as the attacker has the ability to manipulate the blockchain by reversing transactions or modifying specific blocks. In the event of such an attack, the security of the blockchain is severely compromised, as the decentralized nature of the system is undermined. The extent of the damage caused by a fifty one percent attack depends largely on the attacker's mining power, with effects ranging from relatively minor disruptions to significant compromises in the block chain's integrity. Key consequences of a fifty one percent attack include:

Delayed New Transactions: Transactions are unable to be confirmed or added to the blockchain in a timely manner, causing delays in processing new blocks.

Network Disruption: The attack can lead to widespread disruptions in the network, making it unreliable and potentially causing users to lose trust in the system.

Reversing Transactions: Fraudulent actors can revert previously completed transactions, potentially double-spending or altering financial records.

The impact of such an attack highlights the vulnerability of blockchain systems, even with their inherent security measures. To mitigate these risks, cybersecurity measures are essential, involving tools and strategies designed to protect against potential intrusions and attacks, ensuring the reliability and stability of the blockchain network. Cybersecurity in this context is vital to safeguard the infrastructure and prevent malicious actors from exploiting the system for their own gain.

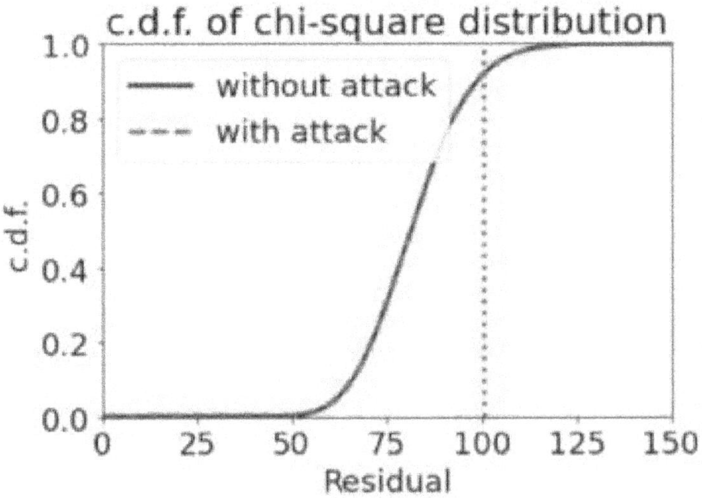

Fig.6.4 CDF of Chi-square distribution attack

The results obtained from the implemented proposal are depicted in Fig.6.5, offering a visual representation of the rates of incorrect events caused by attackers.

Interestingly, the explanation of these outcomes excludes the use of the reputation ratio as a mitigating factor. The graph in Fig.6.5 offers a detailed examination of how well the suggested method works in identifying, stopping, and handling harmful activities in the system. It further highlights the frequency and severity of incorrect events attributed to attackers when reputation-based mechanisms are absent, underscoring the robustness of the proposed method. This visual data serves as a critical tool for evaluating the efficiency of the implementation, providing clear insights into how the system operates under challenging conditions without additional reputation defences. By analyzing the trends and patterns displayed in the graph, stakeholders can assess the solution's resilience and scalability in various attack scenarios. Furthermore, the absence of reliance on a reputation ratio demonstrates the adaptability and independence of the proposed method, which can potentially enhance its application across diverse security-sensitive domains.

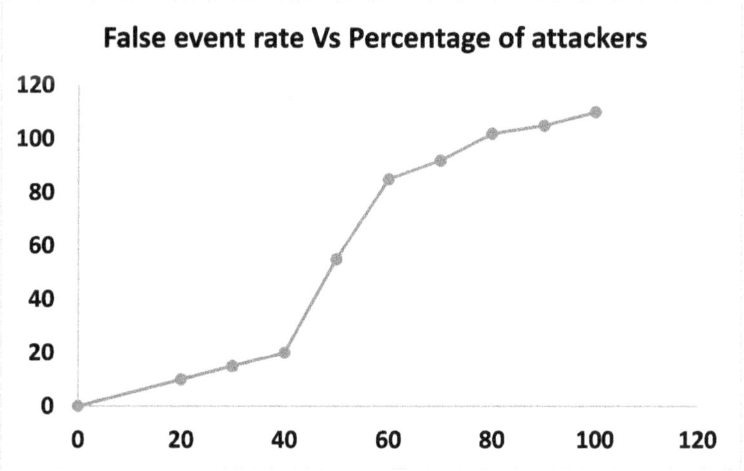

Fig.6.5. False event rate Vs Percentage of attackers

Based on the observable changes in the corresponding percentages, Fig.6.6 demonstrates that incorporating the Reputation Score significantly enhances the system's ability to mitigate the impact of incorrect occurrences. This result underscores the vital role that Reputation Score plays in identifying and neutralizing potential vulnerabilities within the system. By leveraging Reputation Score, the system can effectively prioritize reliable nodes and activities while minimizing the influence of malicious or erroneous events. This improvement is particularly notable in scenarios where high accuracy and trustworthiness are critical, showcasing the practical benefits of integrating Reputation Score into the proposed methodology. The data presented in Fig.6.6 highlights how Reputation Score strengthens the system's resilience by enabling a robust error reduction mechanism. It acts as a safeguard that not only improves decision-making processes but also minimizes adverse outcomes by isolating and reducing the weight of potentially unreliable inputs. Additionally, the emphasis on Reputation Score aligns with modern security frameworks, which rely on trust-based systems to manage complex interactions in distributed environments. This ability to lessen the impact of incorrect occurrences contributes to overall system stability, ensuring that operations remain efficient and secure even in the face of challenges. Such findings affirm the utility of Reputation Score as a pivotal factor in enhancing both the reliability and the robustness of the proposed solution.

Fig.6.6 Success rate Vs Reputation score

The percentages of the number of attackers and the corresponding success rates for two distinct scenarios are depicted in Fig.6.7, providing valuable insights into the The effectiveness of the suggested method. The comparison between the two scenarios highlights the effectiveness of the proposed method in countering attacks and maintaining system integrity. The observed pattern clearly indicates that the proposed solution not only mitigates the impact of attackers but also demonstrates a tangible improvement in terms of operational feasibility and efficiency. This graph really highlights how strong the proposed method is, showing that it can still achieve a high success rate even when there's more attacker activity. The steady performance in different situations shows how adaptable and reliable the approach is, which are really important qualities for secure and scalable systems. Additionally, the findings highlight that the suggested method successfully lowers vulnerabilities, demonstrating its usefulness and relevance in real-world situations. This evidence shows that the proposed solution is a major step forward in tackling the challenges created by malicious entities in distributed systems.

Fig.6.7 Number of attackers and success rate with two cases

Fig.6.8 highlights the relationship between average throughput and latency as the number of participating relays increases, providing a detailed perspective on scalability and performance metrics in the proposed solution. This examination demonstrates how the proposed system efficiently handles an increasing number of relays, maintaining optimal communication performance even under heavy network loads. The analysis further emphasizes the significance of balancing throughput and latency, critical parameters in ensuring smooth operations and robust defenses in cyber-physical systems. The modular architecture of the proposed solution plays a pivotal role in managing overpopulated relay installations, streamlining communication pathways, and enhancing overall network efficiency. This modularity not only supports scalability but also mitigates the risk of bottlenecks, which are often exploited in cyberattacks targeting power grids. By effectively distributing the workload across relays, the system ensures consistent data flow and improved resilience.

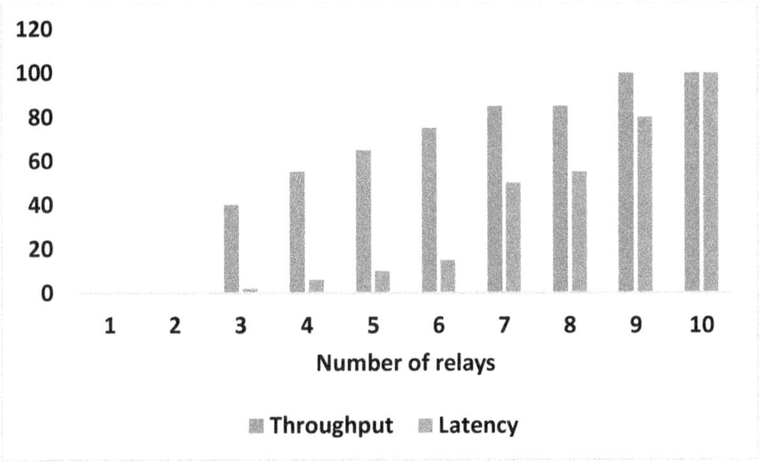

Fig.6.8 Performance vs increasing number of relays

In conclusion, the proposed solution effectively scales to accommodate growing relay density while ensuring that the communication performance remains robust and consistent. The results demonstrate that as the number of relays increases, the system maintains a high level of throughput and low latency, which are crucial for the efficiency and security of the power grid infrastructure. The modular architecture of the solution helps manage relay installations more effectively, reducing congestion and improving how data is distributed across the network. The findings show that using distributed blockchain technology makes the system more resilient to cyber threats, creating a secure and efficient way to communicate for power grid operations.

6.3. Grid-Lock Secure-Chain Consensus Framework

This section looks closely at the outcome, performance analysis, comparison, and discussion to assess how efficient and effective the proposed approach is. The approach used a consensus mechanism based on PoV to create a working smart contract, which was thoroughly tested on the Ethereum network to see how it performs in real-world situations. The performance was benchmarked against traditional consensus mechanisms to highlight PoV's advantages in terms of transaction speed, scalability, and security. Furthermore, the results showed that the PoV-based smart contract outperformed existing systems in terms of reduced latency and improved block generation consistency. These findings underscore the potential of PoV in enhancing blockchain network performance while maintaining decentralization and trust.

6.3.1. Experimental Setup

The proposed method is deployed on a system equipped with 16GB RAM, a 64-bit operating system, and an Intel Core i5-6200U processor, providing adequate computational capacity to support consensus-driven operations in the blockchain environment. This configuration supports the efficient execution and verification of transactions, which are crucial for maintaining the integrity of the blockchain network. The blockchain's role in improving security is particularly evident in its potential to mitigate vulnerabilities present in conventional SCADA systems, the experimental assessment conducted on the IEEE 118 BUS SYSTEM highlights how blockchain technology can enhance the power grid's resilience against cyber-attacks. This work leverages the IEEE 118 BUS SYSTEM to simulate the power grids network's operation and evaluates its performance in the face of potential security threats.

The system comprises key components such as transmission lines, generators, loads, and capacitor banks. A meter is deployed at each node to gather critical analogue data, including current, voltage, and power flow, which are essential for real-time monitoring and decision-making. Every part of the network has a breaker that gathers digital data to evaluate the status of the line, like if it's open or closed. Also, there are two meters set up at the corners of each line to collect both analogue and digital data, including things like power flow, voltage, and current. The data points are really important for keeping an eye on and managing how healthy the network is. Fig.6.9 shows a clear illustration of the IEEE 118 BUS SYSTEM, highlighting how the different components, meters, and branches are set up to gather and send data. This setup helps the system find anomalies and faults, making grid management stronger and more secure while also ensuring the network can withstand cyber threats. This system's use of blockchain technology adds extra security, improving data integrity and making transaction records tamper-proof for smart grid operations.

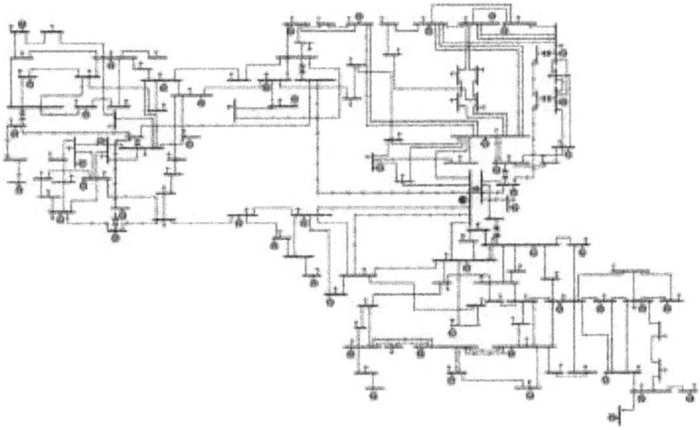

Fig.6.9. IEEE 118 BUS SYSTEM

6.3.2. Performance Analysis

The EPoV consensus method is integrated into the proposed blockchain architecture to evaluate how effective the IEEE 118 BUS SYSTEM is. This method is chosen because it efficiently provides secure and decentralised decision-making, which fits the needs of power grid networks really well. The time it takes to successfully mine a block is selected as the main indicator for performance evaluation. This metric shows how effectively the blockchain architecture works in the specific conditions of the IEEE 118 BUS SYSTEM. The evaluation shows how measuring block mining time can help us understand the efficiency of the PoV consensus in handling transactions and keeping the blockchain secure. Fig.6.10 shows a visual representation of how the proposed blockchain design performs when applied to the IEEE 118 BUS SYSTEM, highlighting the system's capability to manage the complexities of a real-world power grid network. The graph shows how well the blockchain architecture can scale and respond, especially in terms of the speed at which blocks are validated and added to the chain. The results show important insights into how adopting blockchain technology could improve security and operational efficiency in power grid systems. Also, using E-PoV has been shown to cut down block mining time, which makes transaction verification faster and more efficient than the usual consensus methods. This shows that the E-PoV-based blockchain method can help with real-time, high-performance tasks in important infrastructure systems like power grids.

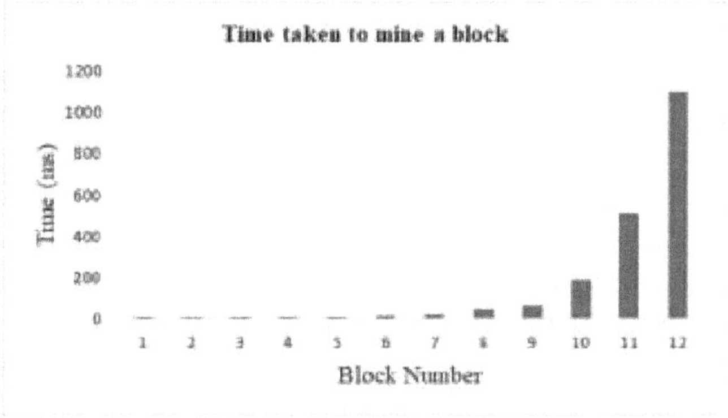

Fig.6.10. Time taken performance for IEEE 118 BUS SYSTEM

Fig.6.10 depicts the mining time for each blockchain block using the PoV consensus mechanism. In the initial phase, blocks 1 to 4 are mined in nearly identical durations, indicating efficient consensus without significant computational overhead. As the block count increases, a gradual rise in mining time is observed, most prominently between blocks 5 and 8, reflecting the increasing complexity of reaching consensus as more blocks are appended. A substantial jump occurs from block 9 onwards—block 9 requires approximately 57 milliseconds, whereas block 12 takes around 1091 milliseconds. This sharp increase results from the cumulative effects of an expanding blockchain, which necessitates additional votes and computational effort to uphold consensus. The trend demonstrates PoV's capacity to maintain a balance between security and performance, as the higher processing demands ensure that only valid blocks are incorporated into the chain. This trend highlights the scalability challenges of blockchain systems, where performance may degrade as the network expands. However, the PoV consensus mechanism effectively mitigates these challenges by optimizing the mining process and reducing the risk of malicious activity, thus maintaining the integrity of the blockchain. The consistent rise in mining time also reflects the increasing complexity of validating and verifying blocks, which strengthens the security of the entire network.

Applied to the IEEE 118-bus system, Fig.6.11 depicts the throughput performance of a blockchain network operating under the EPoV consensus mechanism. Throughput initially increases gradually as relay transactions per second climb from 0 to 100, peaking at around 80 TPS when the rate reaches 50 relay transactions per second. This pattern demonstrates EPoV's capability to maintain a near-linear relationship between transaction rate and throughput, enabling efficient handling of increasing transaction demands in the IEEE 118-bus system. As the relay transaction rate moves from 100 to 150 per second, the throughput climbs more sharply, attaining nearly 130 TPS at 150 relay transactions per second. This trend reflects PoV's effectiveness in sustaining consensus while enabling the system to scale efficiently under higher transaction loads. However, throughput stabilizes at roughly 160 TPS as the relay transaction rate nears 200 per second. Beyond this point, the throughput begins to plateau, suggesting that the system is nearing its maximum capacity for transaction handling within the current configuration. This behavior highlights the PoV method's ability to handle higher transaction loads efficiently but also indicates the potential for diminishing returns as the system is pushed toward its scalability limits. Further optimizations to the consensus mechanism may be necessary to maintain performance as transaction volumes continue to rise.

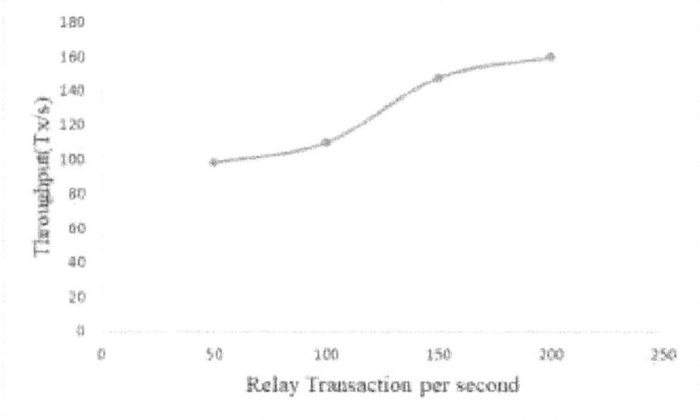

Fig.6.11 Throughput performance for IEEE 118 BUS SYSTEM

Fig.6.12 presents the latency performance for the IEEE 118 BUS SYSTEM, showing a general upward trend where latency changes with increasing relay transaction rates. At lower transaction volumes, latency starts at approximately 0.91 seconds but drops to around 0.2 seconds as the rate approaches 200 transactions per second. This improvement can be attributed to the efficiency of the Proof-of-Vote (PoV) consensus mechanism, which enhances the network's ability to process data and reach agreement quickly. As relay transactions increase, the system becomes more adept at achieving consensus, leading to lower latency and better scalability. Nonetheless, at higher rates, latency gains may plateau due to network congestion and the additional computational effort required for consensus. Even so, PoV maintains effective latency optimization across most operational loads, supporting reliable and responsive performance under heavy demand. Future optimizations in consensus protocols may further enhance latency performance, especially in environments with extremely high transaction volumes.

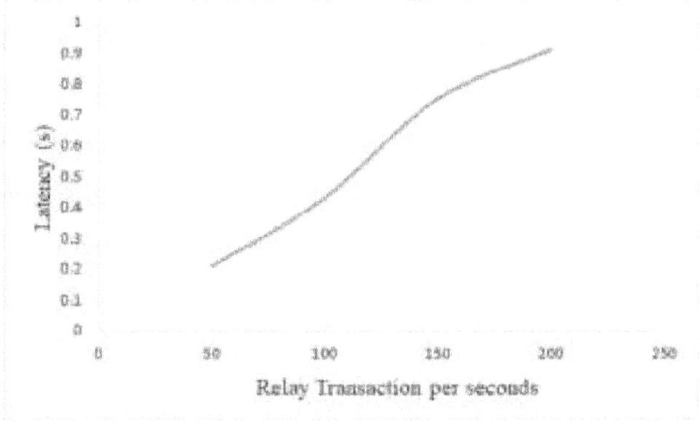

Fig.6.12. Latency performance for IEEE 118 BUS SYSTEM

6.3.3. Performance Comparison

To assess performance in terms of throughput and latency, the proposed approach is compared with existing consensus mechanisms such as PBFT and PoW, considering multiple factors without involving the IEEE 118 BUS SYSTEM. The EPoV method, with its unique approach to consensus, promises improved scalability and efficiency compared to PBFT and PoW, particularly in terms of transaction throughput and system responsiveness. While PBFT provides faster finality and is resistant to certain types of faults, it often faces challenges in scalability as the number of nodes increases, leading to higher latency. In contrast, PoW is known for its robust security, but it suffers from higher computational costs and latency due to the mining process, especially in large-scale systems. Additionally, the EPoV method's lower computational demands and ability to achieve faster consensus could result in lower latency and higher throughput in comparison. By analyzing the performance metrics across these consensus protocols, a more comprehensive understanding of the efficiency and scalability of each approach can be achieved. Moreover, the results of this comparison would shed light on the potential advantages of adopting EPoV in blockchain networks over traditional methods, especially in high-throughput and low-latency environments.

Table 6.2. Comparison of the proposed method with existing method

Consensus Mechanism	Throughput (Tx/s)	Latency(s)
PBFT without IEEE 118 BUS SYSTEM	98	11
PoW without IEEE 118 BUS SYSTEM	120	1
EPoV with IEEE 118 BUS SYSTEM	150	0.89

Table 6.2 shows a comparison of how three consensus mechanisms—PBFT, PoW, and the proposed EPoV—perform when used with the For the IEEE 118 BUS SYSTEM, the assessment measures throughput (transactions per second, Tx/s) and latency (in seconds) for each consensus method. The findings show that the EPoV approach outperforms both PBFT and PoW, achieving a throughput of 150 Tx/s with a latency of 0.89 seconds. In contrast, PBFT records 98 Tx/s with an 11-second latency, while PoW delivers 120 Tx/s with a latency of 1 second. This significant enhancement in both throughput and latency shows how effective EPoV is, especially when looking at the IEEE 118 BUS SYSTEM. The PoV mechanism allows for quicker transaction processing, achieving 150 Tx/s, which is much higher than the slower rates of PBFT and PoW. This speed is really important in settings like power grids, where fast data processing is crucial for keeping the system secure and stable. Also, the lower latency of 0.89 seconds means that transactions happen almost in real time, which is really important for quickly spotting and reacting to possible cyber threats. The comparison shows that the PoV consensus mechanism performs better in terms of throughput and latency compared to traditional methods such as PBFT and PoW. This makes PoV especially fitting for settings such as the IEEE 118 BUS SYSTEM, where quick and effective transaction processing is crucial for ensuring system reliability and security. The noticeable increase in throughput and latency indicates that PoV might be a really effective option for blockchain-based smart grid systems, providing improved real-time data processing and better management of high transaction volumes.

6.4. Conclusion

The results and discussions presented in this chapter highlight the effectiveness of the PoV consensus mechanism and its integration into the Grid-Lock Secure-chain Consensus Framework for ensuring the security and efficiency of electricity power networks. The comparative analysis demonstrates that PoV successfully addresses the limitations of traditional consensus mechanisms like PBFT and PoW by achieving a balance between low latency and high throughput while reducing computational costs and energy consumption. These advantages make PoV particularly suitable for smart grid systems where real-time processing, scalability, and robust security are paramount. Furthermore, the integration of decentralized voting, public and private key encryption, and SHA-256-based ledger protection in the Grid-Lock Framework enhances the resilience of power networks against cyber threats. The innovative division of voting and accounting privileges adds an extra layer of security, safeguarding data integrity and protecting against unauthorized alterations. The performance evaluation using the IEEE 118 BUS SYSTEM confirms the framework's superiority in throughput and latency, establishing its capability to handle the high transaction volumes typical in smart grid environments. This chapter underscores the Grid-Lock Framework's transformative potential in improving the operational stability and security of power systems. While its current implementation demonstrates significant promise, future research should focus on incorporating adaptive algorithms to enhance its performance in dynamic and evolving environments. Furthermore, assessing the framework's scalability for larger, more complex power grids will be crucial for broader adoption and implementation, potentially establishing a new benchmark in smart grid security and operational efficiency.

www.ingramcontent.com/pod-product-compliance
Lightning Source LLC
LaVergne TN
LVHW051922051126
851857LV00021B/2106